THE 100* BEST

Africαn

AMERICAN POEMS

(*but I cheated)

Also by Nikki Giovanni

Poetry

Black Feeling Black Talk/Black
  Judgement
Re: Creation
My House
The Women and the Men
Cotton Candy on a Rainy Day
Those Who Ride the Night Winds
The Selected Poems of Nikki Giovanni
Love Poems
Blues: For All the Changes
Quilting the Black-Eyed Pea: Poems
  and Not Quite Poems
Acolytes
The Collected Poetry of Nikki Giovanni
Bicycles: Love Poems

Prose

Gemini: An Extended Autobiographical
  Statement on My First Twenty-five
  Years of Being a Black Poet
A Dialogue: James Baldwin and Nikki
  Giovanni
A Poetic Equation: Conversations
  Between Nikki Giovanni and
  Margaret Walker
Sacred Cows...and Other Edibles
Racism 101

Edited by Nikki Giovanni

Night Comes Softly: An Anthology of
  Black Female Voices
Appalachian Elders: A Warm Hearth
  Sampler
Grand Mothers: Poems, Reminiscences,
  and Short Stories About the Keepers
  of Our Traditions
Grand Fathers: Reminiscences, Poems,
  Recipes, and Photos of the Keepers
  of Our Traditions
Shimmy Shimmy Shimmy Like My
  Sister Kate: Looking at the Harlem
  Renaissance through Poems

For Children

Spin a Soft Black Song
Vacation Time: Poems
  for Children
Knoxville, Tennessee
The Genie in the Jar
The Sun Is So Quiet
Ego-Tripping and Other Poems for
  Young People
The Grasshopper's Song: An Aesop's
  Fable Revisited
Rosa
Abraham Lincoln and Frederick
  Douglass: An American Friendship
Hip Hop Speaks to Children

THE 100* BEST *African* AMERICAN POEMS

(*but I cheated)

EDITED BY
Nikki Giovanni

FEATURING PERFORMANCES ON CD BY RUBY DEE, NOVELLA NELSON,
NIKKI GIOVANNI, ELIZABETH ALEXANDER, SONIA SANCHEZ, ROBERT HAYDEN,
MARILYN NELSON, AND MANY MORE FRIENDS...

sourcebooks
mediaFusion

Copyright © 2010 by Sourcebooks, Inc. Poet copyrights and permissions listed at back.
Cover and internal design © 2010 by Sourcebooks, Inc.
Cover design by The Book Designers
Cover images © Shutterstock.com
Sourcebooks and the colophon are registered trademarks of Sourcebooks, Inc.

Published by Sourcebooks MediaFusion, an imprint of Sourcebooks, Inc.
P.O. Box 4410, Naperville, Illinois 60567-4410
(630) 961-3900
Fax: (630) 961-2168
www.sourcebooks.com

Library of Congress Cataloging-in-Publication data is on file with the publisher.

Printed and bound in the United States of America.
SB 10 9 8 7 6 5 4 3 2 1

THE 100*BEST *African* AMERICAN POEMS

(*but I cheated)

YOU WON'T FIND JUST 100 POEMS HERE.
READ ON AND FIND OUT WHY.

CD Contents

On the CD

Poetry comes alive when read aloud. In its roots, poetry is a spoken art form, a vibrant method of communication, entertainment, and storytelling. The exclusive audio CD that accompanies this book seeks to capture and preserve a modest portion of that art.

Several of the selections on this disc feature poets reading their own work. We were blessed to have poets Sonia Sanchez, Marilyn Nelson, and Elizabeth Alexander contribute their time and talents. We are also grateful to the Library of Congress for its rich store of archival recordings.

The balance of the readings came together on a unique day in October on the campus of Virginia Tech. On that day, a rare and remarkable collection of performers, poets, and poetry lovers of all stripes created a live performance that is preserved in part here, including all its glorious imperfections and wonderful poetic energy.

Led by the passionate stylings of legendary actresses Ruby Dee and Novella Nelson, and of course by our own muse Nikki Giovanni, many of the poems were performed in front of a small crowd of fortunate witnesses. We are gratefully indebted to all who performed and shared the day, including: Dr. Charles Steger, Val Gray Ward, Kevin McDonald, Terry Papillon, Fred D'Aguiar, Sue Ott Rowlands, Carolyn Rude, Virginia Fowler, Aileen Murphy, Ennis McCrery, Ethel Morgan Smith, Gena Chandler, Linda Dixon, Joanne Gabbin, and Carolyn Dixon. Thanks to Jeff Dalton and his team at Virginia Tech for orchestrating the recording.

In the poetic spirit, we invite you to join these poems both on the page and through the voices of these remarkable contributors.

THE AUNT

Mari Evans / TRACK 1 / READ BY CAROLYN H. DIXON

When your mother dies
your aunt comes in
to make sure your
      ribbons are straight
your hair
      is combed right
and your legs
      are not ashy
and before you know it
you are living at
her house
and every night
instead of your mother
your aunt is handing you
      dinner
and telling you
when
when it is time to go to bed
and pulling the blanket up over your shoulders
and saying "goodnight sunshine"
and sometimes have a smile
      in her voice

That is what an aunt does

This book is dedicated to my aunt, Agnes Marsh
—Nikki Giovanni

Introduction

Poems are like clouds on a June morning or two scoops of chocolate ice cream on a sugar cone in August…something everyone can enjoy. Or maybe poems are your cold feet in December on your lover's back…he is in agony but he lets your feet stay…something like that requires a bit of love. Or could it be that poems are exactly like Santa Claus…the promise, the hope, the excitement of a reward, no matter how small, for a good deed done…or a mean deed from which we refrained. The promise of tomorrow. I don't know. It seems that poems are essential. Like football to Fall, baseball to Spring, tennis to Summer, love Anytime. Something you don't think too much about until it is in Season. Then you deliciously anticipate the perfection.

African American poems are like all other poems: beautiful, loving, provocative, thoughtful, and all those other adjectives I can think of. Poems know no boundaries. They, like all Earth citizens, were born in some country, grew up on some culture, then in their blooming became citizens of the Universe. Poems fly from heart to heart, head to head, to whisper a dream, to share a condolence, to congratulate, and to vow forever. The poems are true. They are translated and they are celebrated. They are sung, they are recited, they are delightful. They are neglected. They are forgotten. They are put away. Even in their fallow periods they sprout images. And fight to be revived. And spring back to life with a bit of sunshine and caring.

These poems, this book, admit I cheated. The idea of *this* and no more would simply not work for me. I needed *these* plus *those*. My mother's favorite poem by Robert Hayden, plus James Weldon Johnson beginning a world that included the longing of the unfree for a loving God. My own fun "Ego Tripping" reaching to embrace Margaret Walker's "For My People." "Train Rides" and "Nikki-Rosa" read by old and loving friends. But also the newness: Novella Nelson lending that sultry voice to the youngsters; Ruby Dee bringing her brilliance to the Gwendolyn Brooks cycle. My Virginia Tech Family wanted to participate: our president Dr. Charles Steger reading "The Negro Speaks of Rivers," recognizing all our souls "have grown deep like the rivers." We celebrate our Hips; we See A Negro Lady at a birthday celebration. Our friends from James Madison University and West Virginia University came to celebrate poetry with us, too. I love these poems so much. The only other thing I would have loved is Caroline Kennedy reading "A Clean Slate."

At the end of a loving day of laughter in Jeff Dalton's studio, when Clinton's makeup had taken forty years off some of us and twenty-five off others, we all came together with one last great cry: the Dean of our College; the Director of Honors; young, old, professional, professor, and recited in one great voice "We Real Cool." Yeah. We are. This book says Poetry Is For Everyone.

What a Treat to be Snowbound with *The 100* Best African American Poems (*but I cheated)*.

I did cheat.

It's true.

But I did not lie.

Nikki Giovanni

Poet

12 December 2009

FOR MY PEOPLE

Margaret Walker / TRACK 2 / READ BY VAL GRAY WARD

For my people everywhere singing their slave songs repeatedly: their dirges and their ditties and their blues and jubilees, praying their prayers nightly to an unknown god, bending their knees humbly to an unseen power;

For my people lending their strength to the years, to the gone years and the now years and the maybe years, washing ironing cooking scrubbing sewing mending hoeing plowing digging planting pruning patching dragging along never gaining never reaping never knowing and never understanding;

For my playmates in the clay and dust and sand of Alabama backyards playing baptizing and preaching and doctor and jail and soldier and school and mama and cooking and playhouse and concert and store and hair and Miss Choomby and company;

For the cramped bewildered years we went to school to learn to know the reasons why and the answers to and the people who and the places where and the days when, in memory of the bitter hours when we discovered we were black and poor and small and different and nobody cared and nobody wondered and nobody understood;

For the boys and girls who grew in spite of these things to be man and woman, to laugh and dance and sing and play and drink their wine and religion and success, to marry their playmates and bear children and then die of consumption and anemia and lynching;

For my people thronging 47th Street in Chicago and Lenox Avenue in New York and Rampart Street in New Orleans, lost disinherited dispossessed and happy people filling the cabarets and taverns and other people's pockets needing bread and shoes and milk and land and money and something— something all our own;

For my people walking blindly spreading joy, losing time being lazy, sleeping when hungry, shouting when burdened, drinking when hopeless, tied and shackled and tangled among ourselves by the unseen creatures who tower over us omnisciently and laugh;

For my people blundering and groping and floundering in the dark of churches and schools and clubs and societies, associations and councils and committees and conventions, distressed and disturbed and deceived and devoured by money-hungry glory-craving leeches, preyed on by facile force of state and fad and novelty, by false prophet and holy believer;

For my people standing trying to fashion a better way from confusion, from hypocrisy and misunderstanding, trying to fashion a world that will hold all the people, all the faces, all the dams and eves and their countless generations;

Let a new earth rise. Let another world be born. Let a bloody peace by written in the sky. Let a second generation full of courage issue forth; let a people loving freedom come to growth. Let a beauty full of healing and strength of final clenching by the pulsing in our spirits and our blood. Let the martial songs be written, let the dirges disappear. Let a race of men now rise and take control.

LEROY

Amiri Baraka (LeRoi Jones)

I wanted to know my mother when she sat
looking sad across the campus in the late 20s
into the future of the soul, there were black angels
straining above her head, carrying life from our ancestors,
and knowledge, and the strong nigger feeling. She sat
(in that photo in the yearbook I showed Vashti) getting into
new blues, from the old ones, the trips and passions
showered on her by her own. Hypnotizing me, from so far
ago, from that vantage of knowledge passed on to her passed on
to me and all the other black people of our time.
When I die, the consciousness I carry I will to
black people. May they pick me apart and take the
useful parts, the sweet meat of my feelings. And leave
the bitter bullshit rotten white parts
alone.

ARS POETICA: NOV. 7, 2008
L. Lamar Wilson

"…a mutt like me" —Barack Obama

I am the what-are-you.
I am the brown, the red, the white, the sometimes blue.
I got some Indian in my family.
I got some cracker, too.
Where I'm from, cracker is a badge
Men wear like nigga in some 'hoods.
I am neither & both just the same.
My family owns the land
On which my family was *Massa* & slave.
The crackers don't claim us anymore.
The niggas never did, too uppity for their shelved lives.
I do not know what tribe I'm from, Indian or African.
My family never thought it important to note,
& I cannot afford Dr. Kittles' tests to answer for the latter yet,
But when I can & his people read my blood,
I'm going back to Africa, just like the crackers
In my parts told me to, to see
If my people there recognize me.

The Mascogos here already reclaimed me,
Though their people voted them away, too.
Although I've lost a lot of melanin
& some of my native tongues, I'm going to offer
My people the ones I've remembered. I'll tell them
 Soy su negro hermano más oscuro.
 Soy vasto. Contengo las multitudes.
They'll understand. I knew that language
Before I knew I knew that language. It came naturally.
So did my crush on my high school teacher, Senor Herrera.
He called me his *hijo*. I never got the nerve
To call him Daddy, except in my dreams.
Sr. Herrera had a nice ass. I am an ass man.
No worries. I have never been a nymphomaniac.
These days, HIV keeps me on an even keel.
You may have thought I didn't know you knew
This truth was coming, but I know you did.

I am often left alone with my thoughts in my one good hand,
With a charge to keep & a god to glorify.
I am mastering the power of positive thinking.
I have had three decades of practice: I learned the power
Of the mind when I ignored my left arm, hanging limp
Like a tattered flag in my pledge of allegiance.
I am your paragon, your darling geisha boy, I said,
With tennis racket, trumpet,
piano, pen, computer keys, backs,
cupped them, held them, watched them walk
away whole & leave me bereft & free.
Whatever the five fingers I could move caressed
Sang notes no one else could reach
& everyone in my path marveled,
Even my crackers & my niggas.
Then one night I met a lawyer,
Another *inteligente* man with a nice ass,
Who said *I can't get fucked by a cripple*.
& I've been trying to un-cripple my mind
Ever since from wondering if Erb's palsy
Is why Johnnie & Jason couldn't
Love me outside our darkened bedrooms' walls.
I speak their names because my god
Doesn't get down on the elliptical tip.

I need to tell you something. I am not
Your paragon, your darling geisha boy. I am not
Here to entertain you. I am not dying.
I am not
Taking those antiretroviral concoctions
Because they are not designed with mutts like me
& Barack & you & you in mind, created
To make us addicts, to fund
An industry hungry for you & you & you
To come in, sit down, rest a little while,
Un-cripple your mind & body of its heavy burdens.
Come in. Lay it all down.

I do not want to be numb. I am not
Afraid of facing you, or me, or the notion
Of we the people anymore.
      I am your darker brother.
      I am vast. I contain multitudes.
I am the what-are-you.
I am the brown, the red, the white, the sometimes blue.
& I am all American.
      What are you?

KA'BA
Amiri Baraka (LeRoi Jones)

"A closed window looks down
on a dirty courtyard, and Black people
call across or scream across or walk across
defying physics in the stream of their will.

Our world is full of sound
Our world is more lovely than anyone's
tho we suffer, and kill each other
and sometimes fail to walk the air.

We are beautiful people
With African imaginations
full of masks and dances and swelling chants
with African eyes, and noses, and arms
tho we sprawl in gray chains in a place
full of winters, when what we want is sun.

We have been captured,
and we labor to make our getaway, into
the ancient image; into a new

Correspondence with ourselves
and our Black family. We need magic
now we need the spells, to raise up
return, destroy, and create. What will be

the sacred word?

WHEN YOU HAVE FORGOTTEN SUNDAY: THE LOVE STORY

Gwendolyn Brooks / TRACK 3 / READ BY RUBY DEE

—And when you have forgotten the bright bedclothes
   on a Wednesday and a Saturday,
And most especially when you have forgotten Sunday—
When you have forgotten Sunday halves in bed,
Or me sitting on the front-room radiator in the limping
   afternoon
Looking off down the long street
To nowhere,
Hugged by my plain old wrapper of no-expectation
And nothing-I-have-to-do and I'm-happy-why?
And if-Monday-never-had-to-come—
When you have forgotten that, I say,
And how you swore, if somebody beeped the bell,
And how my heart played hopscotch if the telephone
   rang;
And how we finally went in to Sunday dinner,
That is to say, went across the front room floor to the
   ink-spotted table in the southwest corner

To Sunday dinner, which was always chicken and
    noodles
Or chicken and rice
And salad and rye bread and tea
And chocolate chip cookies—
I say, when you have forgotten that,
When you have forgotten my little presentiment
That the war would be over before they got to you;
And how we finally undressed and whipped out the
    light and flowed into bed,
And lay loose-limbed for a moment in the week-end
Bright bedclothes,
Then gently folded into each other—
When you have, I say, forgotten all that,
Then you may tell,
Then I may believe
You have forgotten me well.

THE SERMON ON THE WARPLAND
Gwendolyn Brooks

"The fact that we are black is our ultimate reality."
—Ron Karenga

And several strengths from drowsiness campaigned
but spoke in Single Sermon on the warpland.

And went about the warpland saying No.
"My people, black and black, revile the River.
Say that the River turns, and turn the River.

Say that our Something in doublepod contains
seeds for the coming hell and health together.
Prepare to meet
(sisters, brothers) the brash and terrible weather;
the pains;
the bruising; the collapse of bestials, idols.
But then oh then!—the stuffing of the hulls!
the seasoning of the periously sweet!
the health! the heralding of the clear obscure!

Build now your Church, my brothers, sisters. Build
never with brick nor Corten nor with granite.
Build with lithe love. With love like lion-eyes.
With love like morningrise.
With love like black, our black—
luminously indiscreet;
complete; continuous."

WE REAL COOL

Gwendolyn Brooks / TRACKS 4 & 5 / READ BY THE

POET AND BY ENSEMBLE

The Pool Players.
Seven at the Golden Shovel.

We real cool. We
Left school. We

Lurk late. We
Strike straight. We

Sing sin. We
Thin gin. We

Jazz June. We
Die soon.

JAZZ BABY IS IT IN YOU
Antoine Harris

Live Strong, I
Live Long. I

Live meek, I
Die weak, I

Think slow, Yet
Move fast, I

Think first
Finish Last, I

Go away, To
That place, To

Sounds, of
Old Ray, Belting Out

Night and Day, Swing
And sway, to words

That Say, Take
Me Away, from

Every Day, Saxophone
Runs and Baritone, Riffs

Give nigguhs, with no present
A millionaire's gifts

So let Billie's Voice, Lift
And Macio's Horn Blow

To take me from your world
Where all Jazz lovers go.......

UNTITLED

Adam Daniel

I fade into the night with
Nina Simone spinning smooth like honey
disappearing into lucidity
I never cared for the word dreams
for dreams are quite different
than what comes at night
flowing out into all
this lucidity gives liberty
to what awaits
tomorrow is only a dream away.

OLD LEM
Sterling A. Brown / TRACK 6 / READ BY JOANNE V. GABBIN

I talked to old Lem
and old Lem said:
   "They weigh the cotton
   They store the corn
   We only good enough
   To work the rows;
They run the commissary
They keep the books
   We gotta be grateful
   For being cheated;
Whippersnapper clerks
Call us out of our name
   We got to say mister
   To spindling boys
They make our figgers
Turn somersets
We buck in the middle
   Say, 'Thankyuh, sah.'
      They don't come by ones
      They don't come by twos
      But they come by tens.

"They got the judges
They go the lawyers
They got the jury-rolls
They got the law
      They don't come by ones
They got the sheriffs
They got the deputies
      They don't come by twos
They got the shotguns
They got the rope
   We git the justice
   In the end
      And they come by tens.

"Their fists stay closed
Their eyes look straight
   Our hands stay open
   Our eyes must fall
      They don't come by ones
They got the manhood
They got the courage
      They don't come by twos
   We got to slink around
   Hangtailed hounds.
They burn us when we dogs
They burn us when we men
      They come by tens...

"I had a buddy
Six foot of man
Muscled up perfect
Game to the heart
        They don't come by ones
Outworked and outfought
Any man or two men
        They don't come by twos
He spoke out of turn
At the commissary
They gave him a day
To git out the county
He didn't take it.
He said 'Come and get me.'
They came and got him
        And they came by tens.
He stayed in the county—
He lays there dead.

        They don't come by ones
        They don't come by twos
        But they come by tens."

I AM ACCUSED OF TENDING TO THE PAST

Lucille Clifton / TRACK 7 / READ BY SUE OTT ROWLANDS

i am accused of tending to the past
as if i made it,
as if i sculpted it
with my own hands. i did not
this past was waiting for me
when i came,
a monstrous unnamed baby,
and i with my mother's itch
took it to breast
and named it
History.
she is more human now,
learning languages everyday,
remembering faces, names and dates.
when she is strong enough to travel
on her own, beware, she will.

I AM A BLACK WOMAN

Mari Evans / TRACK 8 / READ BY VAL GRAY WARD

I am a black woman
the music of my song
some sweet arpeggio of tears
is written in a minor key
and I
can be heard humming in the night
Can be heard
            humming
in the night

I saw my mate leap screaming to the sea
and I/with these hands/cupped the lifebreath
from my issue in the canebrake
I lost Nat's swinging body in a rain of tears
and heard my son scream all the way from Anzio
for peace he never knew...I
learned Da Nang and Pork Chop Hill
in anguish
Now my nostrils know the gas
and these trigger tire/d fingers
seek the softness in my warrior's beard

I
am a black woman
tall as a cypress
strong
beyond all definition still
defying place
and time
and circumstance
   assailed
       impervious
           indestructible

Look
   on me and be
renewed

WHO CAN BE BORN BLACK?

Mari Evans / TRACK 9 / READ BY NOVELLA NELSON

Who
can be born black
and not
sing
the wonder of it
the joy
the
challenge

And/to come together
in a coming togetherness
vibrating with the fires of pure knowing
reeling with power
ringing with the sound above sound above sound
to explode/in the majesty of our oneness
our comingtogether
in a comingtogetherness

Who
can be born
black
and not exult!

NIKKI-ROSA
Nikki Giovanni / TRACK 10 / READ BY LINDA DIXON

childhood remembrances are always a drag
if you're Black
you always remember things like living in Woodlawn
with no inside toilet
and if you become famous or something
they never talk about how happy you were to have
your mother
all to yourself and
how good the water felt when you got your bath
from one of those
big tubs that folk in chicago barbecue in
and somehow when you talk about home
it never gets across how much you
understood their feelings
as the whole family attended meetings about Hollydale
and even though you remember

your biographers never understand
your father's pain as he sells his stock
and another dream goes
and though you're poor it isn't poverty that
concerns you
and though they fought a lot
it isn't your father's drinking that makes any difference
but only that everybody is together and you
and your sister have happy birthdays and very good
Christmases
and I really hope no white person ever has cause
to write about me
because they never understand
Black love is Black wealth and they'll
probably talk about my hard childhood
and never understand that
all the while I was happy

KNOXVILLE, TENNESSEE

Nikki Giovanni / TRACK 11 / READ BY THE POET

I always like summer
best
you can eat fresh corn
from daddy's garden
and okra
and greens
and cabbage
and lots of
barbeque
and buttermilk
and homemade ice-cream
at the church picnic
and listen to
gospel music
outside
at the church
homecoming
and go to the mountains with
your grandmother
and go barefooted
and be warm
all the time
not only when you go to bed
and sleep

THE DRY SPELL

Kevin Young / TRACK 12 / READ BY NOVELLA NELSON

Waking early
with the warming house
my grandmother knew what to do
taking care not to wake
Da Da   she cooked up a storm
in darkness   adding silent spices
and hot sauce

to stay cool. She ate later, alone
after the children had been gathered
and made to eat
her red eggs. Da Da rose
late, long after
the roosters had crowed
his name, clearing
an ashy throat
pulling on long
wooly underwear
to make him sweat

even more. The fields have gone
long enough without water
he liked to say, so can I
and when he returned
pounds heavier
from those thirsty fields
he was even cooler
losing each soaked
woolen skin
to the floor, dropping
naked rain in his
wife's earthen arms.

THOSE WINTER SUNDAYS

Robert Hayden / TRACKS 13 & 14 / READ BY

CAROLYN RUDE AND BY THE POET

Sundays too my father got up early
and put his clothes on in the blueblack cold,
then with cracked hands that ached
from labor in the weekday weather made
banked fires blaze. No one ever thanked him.

I'd wake and hear the cold splintering, breaking.
When the rooms were warm, he'd call,
and slowly I would rise and dress,
fearing the chronic angers of that house,

Speaking indifferently to him,
who had driven out the cold
and polished my good shoes as well.
What did I know, what did I know
of love's austerc and lonely offices?

FREDERICK DOUGLASS
Robert Hayden

When it is finally ours, this freedom, this liberty, this beautiful
and terrible thing, needful to man as air,
usable as earth; when it belongs at last to all,
when it is truly instinct, brain matter, diastole, systole,
reflex action; when it is finally won; when it is more
than the gaudy mumbo jumbo of politicians:
this man, this Douglass, this former slave, this Negro
beaten to his knees, exiled, visioning a world
where none is lonely, none hunted, alien,
this man, superb in love and logic, this man
shall be remembered. Oh, not with statues' rhetoric,
not with legends and poems and wreaths of bronze alone,
but with the lives grown out of his life, the lives
fleshing his dream of the beautiful, needful thing.

THE NEGRO SPEAKS OF RIVERS

Langston Hughes / TRACK 15 / READ BY DR. CHARLES STEGER

To W.E.B. DuBois

I've known rivers:
I've known rivers ancient as the world and older than the
      flow of human blood in human veins.

My soul has grown deep like the rivers.

I bathed in the Euphrates when dawns were young.
I built my hut near the Congo and it lulled me to sleep.
I looked upon the Nile and raised the pyramids above it.
I heard the singing of the Mississippi when Abe Lincoln
      went down to New Orleans, and I've seen its muddy
      bosom turn all golden in the sunset.

I've known rivers:
Ancient, dusky rivers.

My soul has grown deep like the rivers.

CHOOSING THE BLUES
Angela Jackson

For S. Brandi Barnes

When Willie Mae went down to the barber shop
to visit her boyfriend who cut hair there
I went with her. Walking beside her on the street
the men said hey and stopped to watch her just walk.
Boyfriend Barber cut hair and cut his glance at her
O, he could see the tree for the forest; he pressed
down the wild crest on a man's head and shaved it off
just so he could watch her standing there by the juke
box choosing the blues she would wear for the afternoon.
Right there Little Milton would shoot through the store-
front with the peppermint-stick sentry twirling outside—
"If I didn't love you, baby, grits ain't groceries, eggs
ain't poultry and Mona Lisa was a man."
And every razor and mouth would stop its dissembling
business. And Time would sit down in the barber's chair
and tell Memory poised with its scissors in hand
not to cut it too short, just take a little off the ends.

MY FATHER'S LOVE LETTERS
Yusef Komunyakaa

On Fridays he'd open a can of Jax
After coming home from the mill,
& ask me to write a letter to my mother
Who sent postcards of desert flowers
Taller than men. He would beg,
Promising to never beat her
Again. Somehow I was happy
She had gone, & sometimes wanted
To slip in a reminder, how Mary Lou
Williams' "Polka Dots & Moonbeams"
Never made the swelling go down.
His carpenter's apron always bulged
With old nails, a claw hammer
Looped at his side & extension cords
Coiled around his feet.
Words rolled from under the pressure
Of my ballpoint: Love,
Baby, Honey, Please.

We sat in the quiet brutality
Of voltage meters & pipe threaders,
Lost between sentences...
The gleam of a five-pound wedge
On the concrete floor
Pulled a sunset
Through the doorway of his toolshed.
I wondered if she laughed
& held them over a gas burner.
My father could only sign
His name, but he'd look at blueprints
& say how many bricks
Formed each wall. This man,
Who stole roses & hyacinth
For his yard, would stand there
With eyes closed & fists balled,
Laboring over a simple word, almost
Redeemed by what he tried to say.

THE CREATION

James Weldon Johnson / TRACK 16 / READ BY TERRY L. PAPILLON

A Negro Sermon

And God stepped out on space,
And He looked around and said,
"I'm lonely
I'll make me a world."

And as far as the eye of God could see
Darkness covered everything,
Blacker than a hundred midnights
Down in a cypress swamp.

Then God smiled,
And the light broke,
And the darkness rolled up on one side
And the light stood shining on the other,
And God said, *"That's good!"*

Then God reached out and took the light in His hands,
And God rolled the light around in His hands
Until He made the sun;
And He set that sun a-blazing in the heavens.
And the light that was left from making the sun
God gathered it up in a shining ball
And flung it against the darkness,
Spangling the night with the moon and stars.
Then down between
The darkness and the light
He hurled the world;
And God said, *"That's good."*

Then God Himself stepped down—
And the sun was on His right hand
And the moon was on His left;
The stars were clustered about His head
And the earth was under His feet.
And God walked, and where He trod
His footsteps hollowed the valleys out
And bulged the mountains up.

Then He stopped and looked, and saw
That the earth was hot and barren.
So God stepped over to the edge of the world
And He spat out the seven seas;
He batted His eyes, and the lightnings flashed;
He clapped His hands, and the thunders rolled;
And the waters above the earth came down,
The cooling waters came down.

Then the green grass sprouted,
And the little red flowers blossomed,
The pine tree pointed his finger to the sky,
And the oak spread out his arms,
And the lakes cuddled down in the hollows of the ground,
And the rivers ran to the sea;
And God smiled again,
And the rainbow appeared,
And curled itself around His shoulder.

Then God raised His arm and He waved His hand,
Over the sea and over the land,
And He said, *"Bring forth." "Bring forth."*
And quicker than God could drop His hand
Fishes and fowls
And beasts and birds
Swam the rivers and the seas,
Roamed the forests and the woods,
And split the air with their wings.
And God said, *"That's good."*

Then God walked around,
And God looked around
On all that He had made.
He looked at His sun,
And He looked at His moon,
And He looked at His little stars;
He looked on His world
With all its living things,
And God said, *"I'm lonely still."*

Then God sat down
On the side of a hill where He could think;
By a deep, wide river He sat down;
With His head in His hands,
God thought and thought,
Till He thought, *"I'll make me a man."*

Up from the bed of a river
God scooped the clay;
And by the bank of the river
He kneeled Him down;
And there the great God Almighty
Who lit the sun and fixed it in the sky,
Who flung the stars to the most far corner of the night,
Who rounded the earth in the middle of His hand;
This Great God,
Like a mammy bending over her baby,
Kneeled down in the dust
Toiling over a lump of clay
Till He shaped it in His own image;

Then into it He blew the breath of life,
And man became a living soul.
Amen. Amen.

A NEGRO LOVE SONG
Paul Laurence Dunbar

Seen my lady home las' night,
   Jump back, honey, jump back.
Hel' huh han' an' sque'z it tight,
   Jump back, honey, jump back.
Hyeahd huh sigh a little sigh,
Seen a light gleam f'om huh eye,
An' a smile go flittin' by——
   Jump back, honey, jump back.

Hyeahd de win' blow thoo de pine,
   Jump back, honey, jump back.
Mockin'-bird was singin' fine,
   Jump back, honey, jump back.
An' my hea't was beatin' so,
When I reached my lady's do',
Dat I couldn't ba' to go——
   Jump back, honey, jump back.

Put my ahm aroun' huh wais',
   Jump back, honey, jump back.
Raised huh lips an' took a tase,
   Jump back, honey, jump back.
Love me, honey, love me true?
Love me well ez I love you?
An' she answe'd, "'Cose I do"——
   Jump back, honey, jump back.

LIFT EVERY VOICE AND SING
James Weldon Johnson

Lift every voice and sing
Till earth and Heaven ring,
Ring with the harmonies of Liberty;
Let our rejoicing rise
High as the listening skies,
Let it resound loud as the rolling sea.
Sing a song full of the faith that the dark past has taught us,
Sing a song full of the hope that the present has brought us,
Facing the rising sun of our new day begun
Let us march on till victory is won.

Stony the road we trod,
Bitter the chastening rod,
Felt in the days when hope unborn had died;
Yet with a steady beat,
Have not our weary feet
Come to the place for which our fathers sighed?
We have come over a way that with tears have been watered,
We have come, treading our path through the blood of the slaughtered,
Out from the gloomy past
Till now we stand at last
Where the white gleam of our bright star is cast.

God of our weary years,
God of our silent tears,
Thou who has brought us thus far on the way;
Thou who has by Thy might
Led us into the light,
Keep us forever in the path, we pray.
Lest our feet stray from the places, Our God, where we met Thee,
Lest, our hearts, drunk with the wine of the world, we forget Thee;
Shadowed beneath Thy hand,
May we forever stand.
True to our God,
True to our native land.

GO DOWN DEATH

James Weldon Johnson

A Funeral Sermon

Weep not, weep not,
She is not dead;
She's resting in the bosom of Jesus.
Heart-broken husband—weep no more;
Grief-stricken son—weep no more;
Left-lonesome daughter—weep no more;
She's only just gone home.

Day before yesterday morning,
God was looking down from his great, high heaven,
Looking down on all his children,
And his eye fell on Sister Caroline,
Tossing on her bed of pain.
And God's big heart was touched with pity,
With the everlasting pity.

And God sat back on his throne,
And he commanded that tall, bright angel standing at his right hand:
Call me Death!
And that tall, bright angel cried in a voice
That broke like a clap of thunder:
Call Death!—Call Death!
And the echo sounded down the streets of heaven
Till it reached away back to that shadowy place,
Where Death waits with his pale, white horses.

And Death heard the summons,
And he leaped on his fastest horse,
Pale as a sheet in the moonlight.
Up the golden street Death galloped,
And the hoofs of his horse struck fire from the gold,
But they didn't make no sound.
Up Death rode to the Great White Throne,
And waited for God's command.

And God said: Go down, Death, go down,
Go down to Savannah, Georgia,
Down in Yamacraw,
And find Sister Caroline.
She's borne the burden and heat of the day,
She's labored long in my vineyard,
And she's tired—
She's weary—
Do down, Death, and bring her to me.

And Death didn't say a word,
But he loosed the reins on his pale, white horse,
And he clamped the spurs to his bloodless sides,
And out and down he rode,
Through heaven's pearly gates,
Past suns and moons and stars;
On Death rode,
And the foam from his horse was like a comet in the sky;
On Death rode,
Leaving the lightning's flash behind;
Straight on down he came.

While we were watching round her bed,
She turned her eyes and looked away,
She saw what we couldn't see;
She saw Old Death. She saw Old Death
Coming like a falling star.
But Death didn't frighten Sister Caroline;
He looked to her like a welcome friend.
And she whispered to us: I'm going home,
And she smiled and closed her eyes.

And Death took her up like a baby,
And she lay in his icy arms,
But she didn't feel no chill.
And Death began to ride again—
Up beyond the evening star,
Out beyond the morning star,
Into the glittering light of glory,
On to the Great White Throne.
And there he laid Sister Caroline
On the loving breast of Jesus.

And Jesus took his own hand and wiped away her tears,
And he smoothed the furrows from her face,
And the angels sang a little song,
And Jesus rocked her in his arms,
And kept a-saying: Take your rest,
Take your rest, take your rest.

Weep not—weep not,
She is not dead;
She's resting in the bosom of Jesus.

BETWEEN OURSELVES
Audre Lorde

Once when I walked into a room
my eyes would seek out the one or two black faces
for contact or reassurance or just a sign
I was not alone.
Now walking into rooms of black faces
who would destroy me for any difference
to whom shall my eyes look?
Once it was much easier to know
who were my people.

Yet if we were stripped of all our pretenses
and our flesh was cut away
the sun would bleach all our bones
as white
as the face of my black mother
was bleached white by gold
or Orishala
and how does that measure me?

I do not believe
our wants have made all our lies
holy.

Under the sun on the shores of Elmina
a black man sold the woman who carried
my grandmother in her belly
he was paid with coins of bright yellow
that shone in the evening sun
and in the faces of her sons and daughters.
When I see that brother behind my eyes
his irises are bloodless and without color
his tongue clicks like the yellow coins
tossed up on this shore
where we share the same corner of an alien and corrupted heaven
and whenever I try to eat the words
of easy blackness as salvation
I taste the color of my grandmother's first betrayal.

But I do not whistle his name at the shrine of Shopona
bringing down the juices of death upon him
nor forget Orishala, called god of whiteness
who works in the dark wombs of night
forming the shapes we all wear
so that even cripples and dwarfs and albinos
are sacred worshippers when the boiled corn is offered.
Humility lies in the face of history.
I have forgiven myself for him
for the white meat we all consumed in secret
before we were born
we shared the same meal.

When you impale me upon your lances
of narrow blackness
without listening to my heart speak
mourn your own borrowed blood, your own borrowed visions.
Do not mistake my flesh for the enemy
do not write my name in the dust
before the shrine of the god of smallpox
for we are all children of Eshu
god of chance and the unpredictable
and we each wear many changes inside our skin.

Now armed by old scars that have healed
In many different colours
I look into my own faces
as Eshu's daughter crying
if we do not stop killing the other
in ourselves
the self that we hate
in others
soon we shall all lie
in the same direction
and Eshidale's priests will be very busy
who alone must bury
all those who seek their own death
by jumping up from the ground
and landing upon their heads.

THE UNION OF TWO
Haki R. Madhubuti

For Ife and Jake

What matters is the renewing and long running kinship
seeking common mission, willing work, memory, melody, song.

marriage is an art,
created by the serious, enjoyed by the mature,
watered with morning and evening promises.

those who grow into love
remain anchored
like egyptian architecture and seasonal flowers.

it is afrikan that woman and man join in smile, tears, future.
it is traditional that men and women share expectations,
      celebrations, struggles.
it is legend that the nations start in the family.
it is afrikan that our circle expands.
it is wise that we believe in tomorrows, children, quality.
it is written that our vision will equal the promise.

so that your nation will live and tell your stories accurately,
you must be endless in your loving touch of each other,
your unification is the message,
continuance the answer.

August 7, 1986

BALLAD OF BIRMINGHAM
Dudley Randall

On the Bombing of a Church in Birmingham, Alabama, 1963

"Mother dear, may I go downtown
Instead of out to play,
And march the streets of Birmingham
In a Freedom March today?"

"No, baby, no, you may not go,
For the dogs are fierce and wild,
And clubs and hoses, guns and jail
Aren't good for a little child."

"But, mother, I won't be alone.
Other children will go with me,
And march the streets of Birmingham
To make our country free."

"No, baby, no, you may not go,
For I fear those guns will fire.
But you may go to church instead
And sing in the children's choir."

She has combed and brushed her night-dark hair,
And bathed rose petal sweet,
And drawn white gloves on her small brown hands,
And white shoes on her feet.

The mother smiled to know her child
Was in the sacred place,
But that smile was the last smile
To come upon her face.

For when she heard the explosion,
Her eyes grew wet and wild.
She raced through the streets of Birmingham
Calling for her child.

She clawed through bits of glass and brick,
Then lifted out a shoe.
"O, here's the shoe my baby wore,
But, baby, where are you?"

A POEM TO COMPLEMENT OTHER POEMS
Haki R. Madhubuti

change.
like if u were a match i wd light u into something beautiful. change.
    change.
for the better into a realreal together thing. change, from a make believe
nothing on corn meal and water. change.
change. from the last drop to the first, maxwellhouse did. change.
change was a programmer for IBM, thought him was a brown computer.
    change.
colored is something written on southern outhouses. change.
greyhound did, i mean they got rest rooms on buses. change.
    change.
change nigger.
saw a nigger hippy, him wanted to be different. changed.
saw a nigger liberal, him wanted to be different. changed.
saw a nigger conservative, him wanted to be different. changed.
niggers don't u know that niggers are different. change.
a doublechange. nigger wanted a double zero in front of his name; a license
    to kill,
niggers are licensed to be killed. change. a negro: something pigs eat.
change. i say change into a realblack righteous aim. like i don't play
saxophone but that doesn't mean i don't dig 'trane.' change.
change.

hear u coming but yr/steps are too loud. change. even a lamp post changes
   nigger.
change, stop being an instant yes machine. change.
niggers don't change they just grow. that's a change; bigger & better
   niggers.
change, into a necessary blackself.
change, like a gas meter gets higher.
change, like a blues song talking about a righteous tomorrow.
change, like a tax bill getting higher.
change, like a good sister getting better.
change, like knowing wood will burn. change.
know the realenemy.
change,
change nigger: standing on the corner, thought him was cool. him still
   standing there. it's winter time, him cool.
change,
know the realenemy.
change: him wanted to be a TV star. him is. ten o'clock news.
            wanted, wanted. nigger stole some lemon & lime popsicles,
            thought them were diamonds.
change nigger change.
know the realenemy.

change: is u is or is u aint. change. now now change. for the better change.
   read a change. live a change. read a blackpoem. change. be the
   realpeople.
   change. blackpoems
will change:
know the realenemy. change. know the realenemy. change yr/enemy
   change know the real
change know the real enemy change, change, know the realenemy, the
   realenemy, the real
realenemy change your the enemies/change your change your change your
   enemy change
your enemy. know the realenemy, the world's enemy. know them know
   them know them the
realenemy change your enemy change your change change change your
   enemy change change
change change your change change change.
your
mind nigger.

NO IMAGES
Waring Cuney

She does not know
Her beauty,
She thinks her brown body
Has no glory.

If she could dance
Naked,
Under palm trees
And see her image in the river
She would know.

But there are no palm trees
On the street,
And dishwater gives back no
images.

BETWEEN THE WORLD AND ME
Richard Wright

And one morning while in the woods I stumbled suddenly upon the thing,
Stumbled upon it in a grassy clearing guarded by scaly oaks and elms.
And the sooty details of the scene rose, thrusting themselves between the
   world and me...

There was a design of white bones slumbering forgottenly upon a cushion
   of ashes.
There was a charred stump of a sapling pointing a blunt finger accusingly at
   the sky.
There were torn tree limbs, tiny veins of burnt leaves, and a scorched coil of
   greasy hemp;
A vacant shoe, an empty tie, a ripped shirt, a lonely hat, and a pair of
   trousers stiff with black blood.
And upon the trampled grass were buttons, dead matches, butt-ends of
   cigars and cigarettes, peanut shells, a drained gin-flask, and a whore's
   lipstick;
Scattered traces of tar, restless arrays of feathers, and the lingering smell of gasoline.
And through the morning air the sun poured yellow surprise into the eye
   sockets of a stony skull...

And while I stood my mind was frozen with a cold pity for the life that was
    gone.
The ground gripped my feet and my heart was circled by icy walls of fear—
The sun died in the sky; a night wind muttered in the grass and fumbled
    the leaves in the trees; the woods poured forth the hungry yelping of
    hounds; the darkness screamed with thirsty voices; and the witnesses rose
    and lived:
The dry bones stirred, rattled, lifted, melting themselves into my bones.
The grey ashes formed flesh firm and black, entering into my flesh.
The gin-flask passed from mouth to mouth; cigars and cigarettes glowed,
    the whore smeared lipstick red upon her lips,
And a thousand faces swirled around me, clamoring that my life be burned…

And then they had me, stripped me, battering my teeth into my throat till I
    swallowed my own blood.
My voice was drowned in the roar of their voices, and my black wet body
    slipped and rolled in their hands as they bound me to the sapling.
And my skin clung to the bubbling hot tar, falling from me in limp patches.
And the down and quills of the white feathers sank into my raw flesh, and I
    moaned in my agony.
Then my blood was cooled mercifully, cooled by a baptism of gasoline.
And in a blaze of red I leaped to the sky as pain rose like water, boiling my
    limbs.
Panting, begging I clutched childlike, clutched to the hot sides of death.
Now I am dry bones and my face a stony skull staring in yellow surprise at
    the sun…

THEME FOR ENGLISH B
Langston Hughes

The instructor said,

> Go home and write
> a page tonight.
> And let that page come out of you—
> Then, it will be true.

I wonder if it's that simple?
I am twenty-two, colored, born in Winston-Salem.
I went to school there, then Durham, then here
to this college on the hill above Harlem.
I am the only colored student in my class.
The steps from the hill lead down into Harlem,
through a park, then I cross St. Nicholas,
Eighth Avenue, Seventh, and I come to the Y,
the Harlem Branch Y, where I take the elevator
up to my room, sit down, and write this page:

It's not easy to know what is true for you or me
at twenty-two, my age. But I guess I'm what
I feel and see and hear, Harlem, I hear you:
hear you, hear me—we two—you, me, talk on this page.
(I hear New York too.) Me—who?
Well, I like to eat, sleep, drink, and be in love.

I like to work, read, learn, and understand life.
I like a pipe for a Christmas present,
or records—Bessie, bop, or Bach.
I guess being colored doesn't make me *not* like
the same things other folks like who are other races.
So will my page be colored that I write?
Being me, it will not be white.
But it will be
a part of you, instructor.
You are white—
yet a part of me, as I am a part of you.
That's American.
Sometimes perhaps you don't want to be a part of me.
Nor do I often want to be a part of you.
But we are, that's true!
As I learn from you,
I guess you learn from me—
although you're older—and white—
and somewhat more free.

This is my page for English B.

Harlem Suite

EASY BOOGIE
Langston Hughes

Down in the bass
That steady beat
Walking walking walking
Like marching feet.

Down in the bass
That easy roll,
Rolling like I like it
In my soul.

     Riffs, smears, breaks.

Hey, Lawdy, Mama!
Do you hear what I said?
Easy like I rock it
In my bed!

DREAM BOOGIE
Langston Hughes

Good morning, daddy!
Ain't you heard
The boogie-woogie rumble
Of a dream deferred?

Listen closely:
You'll hear their feet
Beating out and beating out a—

    You think
    It's a happy beat?

Listen to it closely:
Ain't you heard
something underneath
like a—

    What did I say?

Sure,
I'm happy!
Take it away!

    Hey, pop!
    Re-bop!
    Mop!

    Y-e-a-h!

DREAM BOOGIE: VARIATION
Langston Hughes

Tinkling treble,
Rolling bass,
High noon teeth
In a midnight face,
Great long fingers
On great big hands,
Screaming pedals
Where his twelve-shoe lands,
Looks like his eyes
Are teasing pain,
A few minutes late
For the Freedom Train.

HARLEM
Langston Hughes

What happens to a dream deferred?

Does it dry up
like a raisin in the sun?
Or fester like a sore—
And then run?
Does it stink like rotten meat?
Or crust and sugar over—
like a syrupy sweet?

Maybe it just sags
like a heavy load.

Or does it explode?

GOOD MORNING
Langston Hughes

Good morning, daddy!
I was born here, he said,
watched Harlem grow
until colored folks spread
from river to river
across the middle of Manhattan
out of Penn Station
dark tenth of a nation,
planes from Puerto Rico,
and holds of boats, chico,
up from Cuba Haiti Jamaica,
in buses marked New York
from Georgia Florida Louisiana
to Harlem Brooklyn the Bronx
but most of all to Harlem
dusky sash across Manhattan

I've seen them come dark
  wondering
  wide-eyed
  dreaming
out of Penn Station—
but the trains are late.
The gates open—
Yet there're bars
at each gate.

  What happens
  to a dream deferred?

Daddy, ain't you heard?

SAME IN BLUES
Langston Hughes

I said to my baby,
Baby, take it slow.
I can't, she said, I can't!
I got to go!

    There's a certain
    amount of traveling
    in a dream deferred.

Lulu said to Leonard,
I want a diamond ring.
Leonard said to Lulu,
You won't get a goddamn thing

    A certain amount
    of nothing
    in a dream deferred.

Daddy, daddy, daddy,
All I want is you.
You can have me, baby—
but my lovin' days is through.

    A certain
    amount of impotence
    in a dream deferred.

Three parties
On my party line—
But that third party,
Lord, ain't mine!

    There's liable
    to be confusion
    in a dream deferred.

From river to river,
Uptown and down,
There's liable to be confusion
when a dream gets kicked around.

ISLAND
Langston Hughes

Between two rivers,
North of the park,
Like darker rivers
The streets are dark.

Black and white,
Gold and brown—
Chocolate-custard
Pie of a town.

Dream within a dream,
Our dream deferred.

Good morning, daddy!

Ain't you heard?

THE BLUE TERRANCE
Terrance Hayes

I come from a long line hollowed out on a dry night,
the first son in a line of someone else's children,
afraid of water, closets, other people's weapons,
hunger and stupidity, afraid of the elderly and the new dead,
bodies tanned by lightening, afraid of dogs without ethos,
each white fang on the long walk home. I believe all the stories
of who I was: a hardback book, a tent behind the house
of a grandmother who was not my grandmother, the smell of beer,
which is a smell like sweat. They say I climbed to the roof
with a box of light bulbs beneath my arm. Before the bricks,
there were trees, before the trees, there were lovers
barely rooted to the field, but let's not talk about them,
it makes me blue. I come from boys throwing rocks
bigger than their fists at the head of the burned girl,
her white legs webbed as lace on a doily. In someone's garage
there was a flashlight on two dogs pinched in heat.
And later, a few of the puppies born dead and too small
to be missed. I come from howls sent up all night and all day,
summers below the hoop and board nailed to a pine tree.

I come from light bulbs glowing with no light and no expressions,
thrown as far as the will allows like a night chore, like a god
changing his mind; from the light broken on the black road
leading to my mother. Tell me what you remember of her
now that her walk is old, now that the bone in her hip strains
to heal its fracture? I come from the hot season
gathering its things and leaving. I come from the dirt road
leading to the paved one. I will not return to the earth
as if I had never been born. I will not wait to become a bird
dark enough to bury itself in midair. I wake up sometimes
in the middle of the country with fur on my neck.
Where did they bury my dog after she hung herself,
and into the roots of what tree are those bones entangled?
I come blessed like a river of black rock, like a long secret,
and the kind of kindness like a door that is closed
but not locked. Yesterday I was nothing but a road
heading four ways. When I threatened to run away
my mother said she would take me where ever I wanted to go.

THE MOTHER
Gwendolyn Brooks / TRACK 17 / READ BY RUBY DEE

Abortions will not let you forget.
You remember the children you got that you did not get,
The damp small pulps with a little or with no hair,
The singers and workers that never handled the air.
You will never neglect or beat
Them, or silence or buy with a sweet.
You will never wind up the sucking-thumb
Or scuttle off ghosts that come.
You will never leave them, controlling your luscious sigh,
Return for a snack of them, with gobbling mother-eye.

I have heard in the voices of the wind the voices of my dim killed children.
I have contracted. I have eased
My dim dears at the breasts they could never suck.
I have said, Sweets, if I sinned, if I seized
Your luck
And your lives from your unfinished reach,
If I stole your births and your names,
Your straight baby tears and your games,
Your stilted or lovely loves, your tumults, your marriages, aches, and your
    deaths,
If I poisoned the beginnings of your breaths,
Believe that even in my deliberateness I was not deliberate.
Though why should I whine,
Whine that the crime was other than mine?—
Since anyhow you are dead.
Or rather, or instead,
You were never made.
But that too, I am afraid,
Is faulty: oh, what shall I say, how is the truth to be said?
You were born, you had body, you died.
It is just that you never giggled or planned or cried.

Believe me, I loved you all.
Believe me, I knew you, though faintly, and I loved, I loved you
All.

A BRONZEVILLE MOTHER LOITERS IN MISSISSIPPI. MEANWHILE, A MISSISSIPPI MOTHER BURNS BACON

Gwendolyn Brooks / TRACK 18 / READ BY RUBY DEE AND NIKKI GIOVANNI

From the first it had been like a
Ballad. It had the beat inevitable. It had the blood.
A wildness cut up, and tied in little bunches,
Like the four-line stanzas of the ballads she had never quite
Understood—the ballads they had set her to, in school.

Herself: the milk-white maid, the "maid mild"
Of the ballad. Pursued
By the Dark Villain. Rescued by the Fine Prince.
The Happiness-Ever-After.
That was worth anything.
It was good to be a "maid mild."
That made the breath go fast.

Her bacon burned. She
Hastened to hide it in the step-on can, and
Drew more strips from the meat case. The eggs and sour-milk biscuits
Did well. She set out a jar
Of her new quince preserve.

…But there was something about the matter of the Dark Villain.
He should have been older, perhaps.
The hacking down of a villain was more fun to think about
When his menace possessed undisputed breadth, undisputed height,
And a harsh kind of vice
And best of all, when history was cluttered
With the bones of many eaten knights and princesses.

The fun was disturbed, then all but nullified
When the Dark Villain was a blackish child
Of fourteen, with eyes still too young to be dirty,
And a mouth too young to have lost every reminder
Of its infant softness.

That boy must have been surprised! For
These were grown-ups. Grown-ups were supposed to be wise.
And the Fine Prince—and that other—so tall, so broad, so
Grown! Perhaps the boy had never guessed
That the trouble with grown-ups was that under the magnificent shell of
   adulthood, just under,
Waited the baby full of tantrums.
It occurred to her that there may have been something
Ridiculous to the picture of the Fine Prince
Rushing (rich with the breadth and height and
Mature solidness whose lack, in the Dark Villain, was impressing her,
Confronting her more and more as this first day after the trial
And acquittal wore on) rushing
With his heavy companion to hack down (unhorsed)
That little foe.
So much had happened, she could not remember now what that foe had
   done
Against her, or if anything had been done.
The one thing in the world that she did know and knew
With terrifying clarity was that her composition
Had disintegrated. That, although the pattern prevailed,
The breaks were everywhere. That she could think
Of no thread capable of the necessary
Sew-work.

She made the babies sit in their places at the table.

Then, before calling Him, she hurried

To the mirror with her comb and lipstick. It was necessary

To be more beautiful than ever.

The beautiful wife.

For sometimes she fancied he looked at her as though

Measuring her. As if he considered, Had she been worth It?

Had *she* been worth the blood, the cramped cries, the little stuttering bravado,

The gradual dulling of those Negro eyes,

The sudden, overwhelming *little-boyness* in that barn?

Whatever she might feel or half-feel, the lipstick necessity was something
  apart. He must never conclude

That she had not been worth It.

He sat down, the Fine Prince, and

Began buttering a biscuit. He looked at his hands.

He twisted in his chair, he scratched his nose.

He glanced again, almost secretly, at his hands.

More papers were in from the North, he mumbled. More meddling
  headlines.

With their pepper-words, "bestiality," and "barbarism," and
"Shocking."

The half-sneers he had mastered for the trial worked across

His sweet and pretty face.

What he'd like to do, he explained, was kill them all.

The time lost. The unwanted fame.

Still, it had been fun to show those intruders

A thing or two. To show that snappy-eyed mother,

That sassy, Northern, brown-black—

Nothing could stop Mississippi.
He knew that. Big Fella
Knew that.
And, what was so good, Mississippi knew that.
Nothing and nothing could stop Mississippi.
They could send in their petitions, and scar
Their newspapers with bleeding headlines. Their governors
Could appeal to Washington…

"What I want," the older baby said, "is 'lasses on my jam."
Whereupon the younger baby
Picked up the molasses pitcher and threw
The molasses in his brother's face. Instantly
The Fine Prince leaned across the table and slapped
The small and smiling criminal.
She did not speak. When the Hand
Came down and away, and she could look at her child,
At her baby-child,
She could think only of blood.
Surely her baby's cheek
Had disappeared, and in its place, surely,
Hung a heaviness, a lengthening red, a red that had no end.
She shook her head. It was not true, of course.
It was not true at all. The
Child's face was as always, the
Color of the paste in her paste-jar.

She left the table, to the tune of the children's lamentations, which were shriller
Than ever. She
Looked out of a window. She said not a word. *That*
Was one of the new Somethings—
The fear,
Tying her as with iron.

Suddenly she felt his hands upon her. He had followed her
To the window. The children were whimpering now.
Such bits of tots. And she, their mother,
Could not protect them. She looked at her shoulders, still
Gripped in the claim of his hands. She tried, but could not resist the idea
That a red ooze was seeping, spreading darkly, thickly, slowly,
Over her white shoulders, her own shoulders,
And over all of Earth and Mars.

He whispered something to her, did the Fine Prince, something
About love, something about love and night and intention.
She heard no hoof-beat of the horse and saw no flash of the shining steel.

He pulled her face around to meet
His, and there it was, close close,
For the first time in all the days and nights.
His mouth, wet and red,
So very, very, very red,
Closed over hers.

Then a sickness heaved within her. The courtroom Coca-Cola,
The courtroom beer and hate and sweat and drone,
Pushed like a wall against her. She wanted to bear it.
But his mouth would not go away and neither would the
Decapitated exclamation points in that Other Woman's eyes.

She did not scream.
She stood there.
But a hatred for him burst into glorious flower,
And its perfume enclasped them—big,
Bigger than all magnolias.

The last bleak news of the ballad.
The rest of the rugged music.
The last quatrain.

THE LAST QUATRAIN OF THE BALLAD OF EMMETT TILL
Gwendolyn Brooks

after the murder,
after the burial

Emmett's mother is a pretty-faced thing;
  the tint of pulled taffy.
She sits in a red room,
  drinking black coffee.
She kisses her killed boy.
  And she is sorry.
Chaos in windy grays
  through a red prairie.

A SUNSET OF THE CITY
Gwendolyn Brooks / TRACK 19 / READ BY RUBY DEE

Kathleen Eileen

Already I am no longer looked at with lechery or love.
My daughters and sons have put me away with marbles and dolls,
Are gone from the house.
My husband and lovers are pleasant or somewhat polite
And night is night.

It is a real chill out,
The genuine thing.
I am not deceived, I do not think it is still summer
Because sun stays and birds continue to sing.

It is summer-gone that I see, it is summer-gone.
The sweet flowers indrying and dying down,
The grasses forgetting their blaze and consenting to brown.

It is a real chill out. The fall crisp comes.
I am aware there is winter to heed.
There is no warm house
That is fitted with my need.
I am cold in this cold house this house
Whose washed echoes are tremulous down lost halls.
I am a woman, and dusty, standing among new affairs.
I am a woman who hurries through her prayers.

Tin intimations of a quiet core to be my
Desert and my dear relief
Come: there shall be such islanding from grief,
And small communion with the master shore.
Twang they. And I incline this ear to tin,
Consult a dual dilemma. Whether to dry
In humming pallor or to leap and die.

Somebody muffed it? Somebody wanted to joke.

THINGS I CARRIED COMING INTO THE WORLD
Remica L. Bingham

The weight of my parents,
the dawn of them;
my grandmother's lackluster
life; the guilt of my grandfather's mistress
after he'd been scalded with hot
water, tender flesh boiling on his back;
my color, the umber slick of it
deepening over two weeks time,
an aunt worrying it would never stop;
the heart of a boy, whose name
was forgotten before it was given,
who passed me a note in fourth grade
that I spat upon and shot back
in scribbled, torn pieces;
obligation, the bane of memory,
the cleft a loss in 1967 creates
when a mother of mine
two mothers removed, was left
broken on the sidewalk
after a drunk white man
jumped the curve
in the colored neighborhood,
the darkness of the familiar voice
that has to tell me this;

my father's falsetto
before nicotine had its way
with his voice; Jesus and all
his demands; soft hands;
the sight of a woman
at my first funeral, called away
to God, erupted, brought back
in a clapboard church;
the bend of a slow, steady hump
overpowering an uncle's back;
my godson's vermilion face,
the uncertainty of him,
the walk I took with his mother,
past the clinic on through
to the other side;
a fistful of wanting; a blow
to the insides when distance
walks in; the braid of death,
streaked and ribboned against
my family's back, its greedy
interruption, its persistence,
the unwanted strands
of the thick-laced thing.

TOPOGRAPHY
Remica L. Bingham

Tonight   I'm moving,

        traveling beyond modern mumbling

           to a prehistoric groan.

  Before fillers and fidgets

      was the guttural hum,

the soft skin of thigh

         under rough begging hand.

      Before we began paraphrasing want,

there were tongues with purpose, topography

    for mouth and underbelly, dams

for the body's rivers.

           My breasts are tender

    for the wrong reasons—not

        insistent teeth, unyielding

jaw or kneading hand—they ache from the lack

of honest touch.

Keep watching

and I'll open my body like Solomon

serenading Shulamite daughters

of distant lands.

If evidence is

what you want

get the pomegranate wine, choose

any appendage as a reed-brush pen.

Sign here.

BENEATH ME
Jericho Brown

They were of a different hue.
They were all the same color.
The roaches at 51 Felton Street
Went to work when we snored.
They raced for black lines
At the flick of a switch.
They were an athletic sort.
Some of their youngest laughed
At my Chuck Taylor's,
And I just knew
I'd never make it to the Olympics.
Sleep and they'd creep
Into my ears come night.
They conspired with certain spiders
Regarding ladder and crane designs.
Anything to top the refrigerator,
For the loaf of white bread.
They did not fly
Because they chose not to.
They would not sing
Above a roach whisper.

The roaches on Felton ruled
The cabinets, the land
Of pots and plates and pans.
They were well-dressed and polite.
We sneezed. They said
Bless you. They coughed.
We slapped their shiny backs.
But I don't have to miss them
Coursing through the walls
I come from. All that crawls
Beneath me dies
When I try my walk away.
Every time I tell a lie, I smile
And imagine their coupling, oh
God, their loveless orgies.
Insects. Incest. 674 families
Below my family's beds.
The roaches at 51 Felton Street,
They hate my human face.
They know my last name.

AUTOBIOGRAPHY
Jericho Brown

Keep the line steady   keep your back straight
Keep coming
Back for more   keep fucking
With me Cletus
Keep putting your hands on me like that
And you'll always have a place to lay your head
Keep my waistline down   keep your figure up
Keep your man happy   keep a woman crazy
Keep your daddy off your mama
Or next time I'm calling the police
Keep these nappy-headed children
Off my green green grass
Keep talking smart if you want to
Keep looking at my man
And I'll cut you a new eyelid
Keep looking me in my face
When you tell your next lie
Keep on walking I ain't talking to you anymore
Keep holding that last note   keep singing while

I get the splinter out
Keep singing for Jesus baby and everything
Will be alright keep me in your prayers
Keep us in your thoughts   keep your eyes on the black one
He ain't got no sense   keep
Your money in your pocket Nelson
These hos
Giving it away   keep this one
Occupied   I'll get his wallet
Keep on living honey and you'll
Get old too

PARABLE OF THE SOWER
Pamela Sneed

I have nothing in common with George W. Bush
or bible belt conservatives using their votes
to flush away our rights
I have nothing to do with those ungodly government officials
waging wars based on lies and manipulation
responsible for the systematic slaughter of millions
then carrying it out through legislation and bureaucracy
so no one ever sees their bloody hands
I have nothing to do with red state republicans
holding onto visions of old American values
while watching the Jerry Springer show and its usual cast
of transvestite dads, cheating spouses,
while our nation anthem is becoming "It's hard out
here for a pimp!"
which I had occasion to hear recently when the Academy Awards
ripped off BET
and had a brown girl wearing razor sharp pink short
shorts
singing the pimp song
in front of an almost all-White audience
She sang it with such gospel fervor and conviction
I found myself in the end like in church
almost wanting to shout Amen, Hallelujah
but I was even more shocked recently
when I went to the theater to see an avant-garde
performance

and there was a fabulous downtown White woman actress
playing the character of "Emperor Jones" in blackface
a role that pioneering Black actor, Paul Robeson made
famous.
It was a role she first played in 1998
and in an outraged political climate lost all funding
for
but resurrected in 2006
and no one, including myself did anything to stop it
In fact the person in the audience cheering loudest was a Black
man
So, I've got nothing to do with those people
or the evangelical Christians
those can't seem to stop the smirking narcissists
who believe as they do in the Bush White House
that they are messengers carrying out God's will.
I have nothing to do with that
I have long since disavowed any belief in organized
religion
through education dispelled any myth of a great white
father in the sky
I have long since outgrown my Black baptist beginnings
like my lover says upon leaving her childhood home
I grew my wings
but I must admit for a long time in my life
as in Genesis there's been darkness, a void
So I wonder if it matters at all tonight
if it can ever be enough
that every year now for at least 20 or 30

I have sat down and written out my stories and poems
I have never really successfully bowed my head
or stayed focused
but I had an idea in my mind that every entry I made
every poem
story penned was a prayer
and like Celie in Alice Walker's novel
The Color Purple
with no particular audience in mind
each letter I wrote-was an instrument
and through them
only through them
I could talk to God
I wonder if that's enough
I wonder if I've always thought a little like Octavia Butler's girl
heroine
in *Parable of the Sower*
what I extracted from it
was if God didn't exist
if the world were an empty palette
I could create her
that we could think of God as a practice
not a person
as action
change.
I know that after 9/11 things got so bad in this
country
when we went to war
as a professor in the college classroom

I decided in certain respects to throw away the textbook
started teaching from my heart
wanted to be like Martin Luther King
to use any opportunity as a platform and pulpit
to speak out
I wanted to be able to say in the end
I stood up for something
I became an antiwar activist
critical of our government
I talked about America's apartheid education
2nd, 3rd class citizenship
I asked my students to think critically
so maybe the religion thing hasn't worked out for me
but I in my heart
I've come to know and practice God.

HERITAGE
Countee Cullen

(For Harold Jackman)

What is Africa to me:
Copper sun or scarlet sea,
Jungle star or jungle track,
Strong bronzed men, or regal black
Women from whose loins I sprang
When the birds of Eden sang?
One three centuries removed
From the scenes his fathers loved,
Spicy grove, cinnamon tree,
What is Africa to me?

So I lie, who all day long
Want no sound except the song
Sung by wild barbaric birds
Goading massive jungle herds,
Juggernauts of flesh that pass
Trampling tall defiant grass
Where young forest lovers lie,
Plighting troth beneath the sky.

So I lie, who always hear,
Though I cram against my ear
Both my thumbs, and keep them there,
Great drums throbbing through the air.
So I lie, whose fount of pride,
Dear distress, and joy allied,
Is my somber flesh and skin,
With the dark blood dammed within
Like great pulsing tides of wine
That, I fear, must burst the fine
Channels of the chafing net
Where they surge and foam and fret.

Africa? A book one thumbs
Listlessly, till slumber comes.
Unremembered are her bats
Circling through the night, her cats
Crouching in the river reeds,
Stalking gentle flesh that feeds
By the river brink; no more
Does the bugle-throated roar
Cry that monarch claws have leapt
From the scabbards where they slept.
Silver snakes that once a year
Doff the lovely coats you wear,
Seek no covert in your fear
Lest a mortal eye should see;
What's your nakedness to me?
Here no leprous flowers rear
Fierce corollas in the air;
Here no bodies sleek and wet,

Dripping mingled rain and sweat,
Tread the savage measures of
Jungle boys and girls in love.
What is last year's snow to me,
Last year's anything? The tree
Budding yearly must forget
How its past arose or set—
Bough and blossom, flower, fruit,
Even what shy bird with mute
Wonder at her travail there,
Meekly labored in its hair.
One three centuries removed
From the scenes his fathers loved,
Spicy grove, cinnamon tree,
What is Africa to me?

So I lie, who find no peace
Night or day, no slight release
From the unremittent beat
Made by cruel padded feet
Walking through my body's street.
Up and down they go, and back,
Treading out a jungle track.
So I lie, who never quite
Safely sleep from rain at night—
I can never rest at all
When the rain begins to fall;
Like a soul gone mad with pain
I must match its weird refrain;
Ever must I twist and squirm,
Writhing like a baited worm,

While its primal measures drip
Through my body, crying, "Strip!
Doff this new exuberance.
Come and dance the Lover's Dance!"
In an old remembered way
Rain works on me night and day.

Quaint, outlandish heathen gods
Black men fashion out of rods,
Clay, and brittle bits of stone,
In a likeness like their own,
My conversion came high-priced;
I belong to Jesus Christ,
Preacher of Humility;
Heathen gods are naught to me.

Father, Son, and Holy Ghost,
So I make an idle boast;
Jesus of the twice-turned cheek,
Lamb of God, although I speak
With my mouth thus, in my heart
Do I play a double part.
Ever at Thy glowing altar
Must my heart grow sick and falter,
Wishing He I served were black,
Thinking then it would not lack
Precedent of pain to guide it,
Let who would or might deride it;
Surely then this flesh would know
Yours had borne a kindred woe.
Lord, I fashion dark gods, too,

Daring even to give You
Dark despairing features where,
Crowned with dark rebellious hair,
Patience wavers just so much as
Mortal grief compels, while touches
Quick and hot, of anger, rise
To smitten cheek and weary eyes.
Lord, forgive me if my need
Sometimes shapes a human creed.

All day long and all night through,
One thing only must I do:
Quench my pride and cool my blood,
Lest I perish in the flood,
Lest a hidden ember set
Timber that I thought was wet
Burning like the dryest flax,
Melting like the merest wax,
Lest the grave restore its dead.
Not yet has my heart or head
In the least way realized
They and I are civilized.

YET DO I MARVEL

Countee Cullen / TRACK 20 / READ BY KEVIN G. McDONALD

I doubt not God is good, well-meaning, kind.
And did He stoop to quibble could tell why
The little buried mole continues blind,
Why flesh that mirrors Him must some day die,
Make plain the reason tortured Tantalus
Is baited by the fickle fruit, declare
If merely brute caprice dooms Sisyphus
To struggle up a never-ending stair.
Inscrutable His ways are, and immune
To catechism by a mind too strewn
With petty cares to slightly understand
What awful brain compels His awful hand.
Yet do I marvel at this curious thing:
To make a poet black, and bid him sing!

INCIDENT
Countee Cullen / TRACK 21 / READ BY GENA E. CHANDLER

(For Eric Walrond)

Once riding in old Baltimore,
   Heart-filled, head-filled with glee,
I saw a Baltimorean
   Keep looking straight at me.

Now I was eight and very small,
   And he was no whit bigger,
And so I smiled, but he poked out
   His tongue and called me, "Nigger."

I saw the whole of Baltimore
   From May until December;
Of all the things that happened there
   That's all that I remember.

WE WEAR THE MASK

Paul Laurence Dunbar / TRACK 22 / READ BY NOVELLA NELSON

We wear the mask that grins and lies,
It hides our cheeks and shades our eyes,—
This debt we pay to human guile;
With torn and bleeding hearts we smile,
And mouth with myriad subtleties.

Why should the world be overwise,
In counting all our tears and sighs?
Nay, let them only see us, while
        We wear the mask.

We smile, but, O great Christ, our cries
To thee from tortured souls arise.
We sing, but oh the clay is vile
Beneath our feet, and long the mile;
But let the world dream otherwise,
        We wear the mask!

TRIFLE
Georgia Douglas Johnson

Against the day of sorrow
Lay by some trifling thing
A smile, a kiss, a flower
For sweet remembering.

Then when the day is darkest
Without one rift of blue
Take out your little trifle
And dream your dream anew.

THE HEART OF A WOMAN
Georgia Douglas Johnson / TRACK 23 / READ BY ETHEL MORGAN SMITH

The heart of a woman goes forth with the dawn,
As a lone bird, soft winging, so restlessly on,
Afar o'er life's turrets and vales does it roam
In the wake of those echoes the heart calls home.

The heart of a woman falls back with the night,
And enters some alien cage in its plight,
And tries to forget it has dreamed of the stars
While it breaks, breaks, breaks on the sheltering bars.

WOMAN WITH FLOWER
Naomi Long Madgett

I wouldn't coax the plant if I were you.
Such watchful nurturing may do it harm.
Let the soil rest from so much digging
And wait until it's dry before you water it.
The leaf's inclined to find its own direction;
Give it a chance to seek the sunlight for itself.

Much growth is stunted by too careful prodding,
Too eager tenderness.
The things we love we have to learn to leave alone.

THE IDEA OF ANCESTRY
Etheridge Knight

1

Taped to the wall of my cell are 47 pictures: 47 black
faces: my father, mother, grandmothers (1 dead), grand
fathers (both dead), brothers, sisters, uncles, aunts,
cousins (1st & 2nd), nieces, and nephews. They stare
across the space at me sprawling on my bunk. I know
their dark eyes, they know mine. I know their style,
they know mine. I am all of them, they are all of me;
they are farmers, I am a thief, I am me, they are thee.

I have at one time or another been in love with my mother,
1 grandmother, 2 sisters, 2 aunts (1 went to the asylum),
and 5 cousins. I am now in love with a 7 yr old niece
(she sends me letters written in large block print, and
her picture is the only one that smiles at me).

I have the same name as 1 grandfather, 3 cousins, 3 nephews,
and 1 uncle. The uncle disappeared when he was 15, just took
off and caught a freight (they say). He's discussed each year
when the family has a reunion, he causes uneasiness in
the clan, he is an empty space. My father's mother, who is 93
and who keeps the Family Bible with everybody's birth dates
(and death dates) in it, always mentions him. There is
no place in her Bible for "whereabouts unknown."

2

Each fall the graves of my grandfathers call me, the brown
hills and red gullies of mississippi send out their electric
messages, galvanizing my genes. Last yr/like a salmon quitting
the cold ocean—leaping and bucking up his birthstream/I
hitchhiked my way from L.A. with 16 caps in my pocket and a
monkey on my back. and I almost kicked it with the kinfolks.
I walked barefooted in my grandmother's backyard/I smelled the
          old
land and the woods/I sipped cornwhiskey from fruit jars with the
          men/
I flirted with the women/I had a ball till the caps ran out
and my habit came down. That night I looked at my grandmother
and split/my guts were screaming for junk/but I was almost
contented/I had almost caught up with me.
(The next day in Memphis I cracked a croaker's crib for a fix.)

This yr there is a gray stone wall damming my stream, and when
the falling leaves stir my genes, I pace my cell or flop on my bunk
and stare at 47 black faces across the space. I am all of them,
they are all of me, I am me, they are thee, and I have no sons
to float in the space between.

DON'T SAY GOODBYE TO THE PORKPIE HAT
Larry Neal

Mingus, Bird, Prez, Langston, and them

Don't say goodbye to the Porkpie Hat that rolled
along on padded shoulders
      that swang bebop phrases
      in Minton's jelly roll dreams
Don't say goodbye to hip hats tilted in the style of a soulful
   era;
the Porkpie Hat that Lester dug
swirling in the sound of sax blown suns
      phrase on phrase, repeating bluely
      tripping in an under crashing
      hi-hat cymbals, a fickle girl
      getting sassy on the rhythms.
Musicians heavy with memories
move in and out of this gloom;
the Porkpie Hat reigns supreme
smell of collard greens
and cotton madness
commingled in the nigger elegance of the style.
      The Porkpie Hat sees tonal memories
      of salt peanuts and hot house birds
      the Porkpie Hat sees…
Cross riffing square kingdoms, riding midnight Scottsboro

trains. We are haunted by the lynched limbs.
On the road:
It would be some hoodoo town
It would be some cracker place
you might meet redneck lynchers
face to face
but mostly you meet mean horn blowers
running obscene riffs
Jelly Roll spoke of such places:
the man with the mojo hand
the dyke with the .38
the yaller girls
and the knifings.

Stop-time Buddy and Creole Sydney
wailed in here. Stop time.
chorus repeats, stop and shuffle.
stop and stomp.
listen to the horns, ain't they mean?
now   ain't they mean
in blue
in blue
in blue streaks of mellow wisdom
blue notes
coiling around
the Porkpie Hat
and ghosts of dead musicians drifting through
here on riffs that smack
of one-leg trumpet players
and daddy glory piano ticklers
who

twisted arpeggios
with diamond-flashed fingers.
There was Jelly Roll Morton, the sweet mackdaddy,
hollering Waller, and Willie The Lion Smith—
some mean showstoppers.

Ghosts of dead holy rollers ricocheted in the air funky
with white lightnin' and sweat.
Emerald bitches shot shit in a kitchen smelling
of funerals and fried chicken.
Each city had a different sound:
there was Mambo, Rhega, Jeanne;
holy the voice of the righteous sisters.

Shape to shape, horn to horn
the Porkpie Hat resurrected himself
night to night, from note to note
skimming the horizons, flashing bluegreenyellow lights
and blowing black stars
and weird looneymoon changes; chords coiled about him
and he was flying
fast
zipping
past
sound
into cosmic silences.

And yes
and caresses flowed from the voice in the horn in the blue
of the yellow whiskey room where bad hustlers with big
coats moved, digging the fly sister, fingerpopping while
tearing at chicken and waffles.

The Porkpie Hat loomed specter like, a vision for the world;
shiny, the knob toe shoes,
sporting hip camel coats
and righteous pin stripes—
pants pressed razor shape;
and caressing his horn, baby like.

So we pick up our axes and prepare
to blast the white dream;
we pick up our axes
re-create ourselves and the universe,
sounds splintering the deepest regions
of spiritual space
crisp and moaning voices
leaping in the horns of destruction,
blowing death and doom to all who have no use for the spirit.

So we cook out of sight
into cascading motions of joy delight
shooflies the Bird lolligagging
and laughing for days,
and the rhythms way up in there
wailing, sending scarlet rays, luminescent,
spattering bone and lie.
we go on cool lords
wailing on into star nights,
rocking whole worlds, unfurling song on song
into long stretches of green spectral shimmerings,
blasting on, fucking the moon with the blunt edge
of a lover's tune, out there now, joy rifting

for days and do
railriding and do
talking some lovely shit and do
to the Blues God who blesses us.

No, don't say goodbye to the Porkpie Hat—
he lives, oh yes.

Lester lives and leaps
Delancey's dilemma is over
Bird lives
Lady lives
Eric stands next to me
while I finger the Afro-horn
Bird lives
Lady lives
Lester leaps in every night
Tad's delight
is mine now
Dinah knows
Richie knows
that Bud is Buddha
that Jelly Roll dug juju
and Lester lives
in Ornette's leapings
the Blues God lives

we live
live
spirit lives
and sound lives
bluebird lives
lives and leaps
dig the mellow voices
dig the Porkpie Hat
dig the spirit in Sun Ra's sound
dig the cosmic Trane
dig be
dig be
dig be
spirit lives in sound
dig be
sound lives in spirit
dig be
yeah!!!
spirit lives
spirit lives
spirit lives
SPIRIT!!!
SWHEEEEEEEEEEEEEEEETT!!!

take it again
this time from the top

CLEANING
Camille T. Dungy

I learned regret at Mother's sink,
jarred tomatoes, river-mud brown,
a generation old, lumping
down the drain. Hating wasted space,
I had discarded what I could
not understand. I hadn't known
a woman to fight drought or frost
for the promise of winter meals,
hadn't known my great-grandmother,
or what it was to have then lose
the company of that woman
who, upon seeing her namesake,
child of her child, grown and gliding
into marriage, gifted the fruit
of her garden, a hard-won strike
against want. Opening the jar,
I knew nothing of the rotting
effect, the twisting grip of years
spent packing, of years spent moving,
further each time, from known comforts:
a grandmother's garden, her rows
always neat, the harvest: bright wealth
mother hoarded. I understood
only the danger of a date
so old. Understanding clearly
what is fatal to the body,
I only understood too late
what can be fatal to the heart.

BOSTON YEAR
Elizabeth Alexander / TRACK 24 / READ BY THE POET

My first week in Cambridge a car full of white boys
tried to run me off the road, and spit through the window,
open to ask directions. I was always asking directions
and always driving: to an Armenian market
in Watertown to buy figs and string cheese, apricots,
dark spices and olives from barrels, tubes of paste
with unreadable Arabic labels. I ate
stuffed grape leaves and watched my lips swell in the mirror.
The floors of my apartment would never come clean.
Whenever I saw other colored people
in bookshops, or museums, or cafeterias, I'd gasp,
smile shyly, but they'd disappear before I spoke.
What would I have said to them? Come with me? Take
me home? Are you my mother? No. I sat alone
in countless Chinese restaurants eating almond
cookies, sipping tea with spoons and spoons of sugar.
Popcorn and coffee was dinner. When I fainted
from migraine in the grocery store, a Portuguese
man above me mouthed: "No breakfast." He gave me
orange juice and chocolate bars. The color red
sprang into relief singing Wagner's *Walküre*.
Entire tribes gyrated and drummed in my head.
I learned the samba from a Brazilian man
so tiny, so festooned with glitter I was certain
that he slept inside a filigreed, Fabergé egg.
No one at the door: no salesmen, Mormons, meter
readers, exterminators, no Harriet Tubman,
no one. Red notes sounding in a grey trolley town.

SHE WEARS RED

Jackie Warren-Moore

She bangs hard on the door
just outside my consciousness
this wild woman I am becoming
"Let me in, open up!" she screams
wearing a long blue dress
of dreams I discarded

I try to ignore her
go about everyday duties
a list that must be followed
she keeps showing me new ways
  to be me
lessons I forgot
she wears red and says
she is staking a claim to beautiful
drops people like bad habits
cutting hurt from her body
carving a new switch to her step
"More bounce to the ounce" she says
"More cushin' for the pushin'"
she is a vulgar girl
knows just what she wants
throws her head back
and laughs out loud

She is something
this new girl I almost was
"Open up" she says
"Be me again
be the girl you were afraid of
wear red again
wear your hair down
black and grey hair you earned
with all the passion you stored inside,
Open up" she says
this wild woman
I am becoming
"Open up
and welcome
this woman
we are"

Yes, the body remembers
when the brain wishes to forget
this snatch of song hummed up
from the back of your past

the 'times they are a changin'
or a certain whir in the atmosphere
the way the air hits the shin
a certain jig in the walk
a step that reminds us
of all we lost to time
sickness and ignorance

the body remembers, all the way to the bone
pain
pleasure
etched into the marrow

slick glide of time over lives
connected by threads
we are too blind to see
too sophisticated to acknowledge

the body remembers
quick flash of tingle
in the back to synapse
tiny pause-between conscious thought
feelings surface
the body asserts
come back, come back, come back
to the feeling
let the body remember
feel again
all she has forgotten
all she continues
to hold on to
yes, she remembers

COMMERCIAL BREAK: ROAD-RUNNER, UNEASY
Tim Seibles

If I didn't know better I'd say
the sun never moved ever,

that somebody just pasted it there
and said the hell with it,

but that's impossible.
After awhile you have to give up

those conspiracy theories.
I get the big picture. I mean,

how big can the picture be?
I actually think it's kind of funny—

that damn coyote always scheming,
always licking his skinny chops

and me, pure speed, the object of all
his hunger, the *everything* he needs—

talk about **impossible**, talk about
the grass is always greener…

I am the other side of the fence.

You've got to wonder, at least a little,
if this could be a set-up:

with all the running I do—
the desert, the canyons, the hillsides, the desert—

all this open road has got to
lead somewhere else. I mean,

that's what freedom's all about, right?
Ending up where you want to be.

I used to think it was funny—*Road-runner*
the coyote's after you Road-runner...

Now, I'm mainly tired. Not that
you'd ever know. I mean,

I can still make the horizon
in two shakes of a snake's tongue,
but it never gets easier out here, alone
with Mr. Big Teeth and his ACME supplies:

leg muscle vitamins, tiger traps,
instant tornado seeds.

C'mon! I'm no tiger.
And who's making all this stuff?

I can't help being a little uneasy.
I do one of my tricks,

a rock-scorching, razor turn at 600 miles an hour
and he falls off the cliff, the coyote—

he really falls: I see the small explosion,
his body slamming into dry dirt

so far down in the canyon
the river looks like a crayon doodle.

That has to hurt, right?
Five seconds later, he's just up the highway

hoisting a huge anvil
above a little, yellow dish of bird feed—

like I don't see what's goin' on. C'mon!

You know how sometimes, even though you're
very serious about the things you do,

it seems like, secretly, there's a
big joke being played,

and you're part of what
someone else is laughing at—only

you can't prove it, so you
keep sweating and believing in

your *career*, as if that
makes the difference, as if somehow

playing along isn't really

playing along as long as you're
not sure what sort of fool

you're being turned into, especially
if you're giving it *100%*.

So, when I see dynamite
tucked under the ACME road-runner cupcakes,

as long as I don't wonder why my safety
isn't coming first in this situation,

as long as I don't think me
and the coyote are actually

working for the same people,

as long as I eat and

get away I'm not really stupid,

right? I'm just fast.

BEFORE MAKING LOVE
Toi Derricotte

I move my hands over your face,
closing my eyes, as if blind;
the cheek bones, broadly spaced,
the wide thick nostrils of the African,
the forehead whose bones push
at both sides as if the horns
of fallen angels lie just under,
the chin that juts forward with pride.
I think of the delicate skull of the Taung child—
earliest of human beings
emerged from darkness—whose geometry
brings word of a small town of dignity
that all the bloody kingdoms rest on.

BE-BOP
Sterling Plumpp

Be-Bop is precise clumsiness.
   Awkward lyricism
   under a feather's control.
A world in a crack.
Seen by ears.
       Von Freeman's
tenor Apocalypses/beginning
skies fussy about air and protective
   of trombones on Jacob's Ladder
   strung from basses
in a comer of handclaps.
Drums praying over evil
   done by trumpets
   and dances in fingertips.
Be-Bop is elusive hammerlocks

a piano accords crescendos
   in blue meanings.
Lingers in beats marching
   across faces of sense.
Harmonic nightmares obeying
   pianissimos of tones
erupting from barks of Powell.
Be-Bop is unexpected
   style punching music
with garlic in tempo,

      Billie's pain
and a cup of insinuations
drunk by laughter
before tears arise.

PERSONAL LETTER NO.3
Sonia Sanchez / TRACK 25 / READ BY THE POET

nothing will keep
us young you know
not young men or
women who spin
their youth on
cool playing sounds,
we are what we
are what we never
think we are.
no more wild geo
graphies of the
flesh, echoes, that
we move in tune
to slower smells.
it is a hard thing
to admit that
sometimes after midnight
I am tired
of it all.

POEM AT THIRTY

Sonia Sanchez / TRACK 26 / READ BY THE POET

it is midnight
no magical bewitching
hour for me
i know only that
i am here waiting
remembering that
once as a child
i walked two
miles in my sleep.
did i know
then where i
was going?
traveling. i'm
always traveling.

i want to tell
you about me
about nights on a
brown couch when
i wrapped my
bones in lint and
refused to move.
no one touches
me anymore.
father do not
send me out
among strangers.
you you black man
stretching scraping
the mold from your body.
here is my hand.
i am not afraid
of the night.

A POEM FOR STERLING BROWN

Sonia Sanchez / TRACK 27 / READ BY THE POET

what song shall i sing you
amid epidemic prophecies
where holy men bleed like water
over the bones of black children?

how shall i call your name
sitting priest/like on mountains
raining incense
scented dancer of the sun?

where shall memory begin you
overturning cradles
rocking cemented eyes
closed flowers
opening like eastern deities under your hand?

and your words.
tall as palm/trees
black with spit
soothing the lacerated mind.

and your words.
scratching the earth
carving dialect men into pyramids
where no minstrel songs
run from their thighs.

your soul, dodging loneliness and
the festivals of Renaissance rhythms
your life
skintight with years
a world created
from love.

you. griot of fire.
harnessing ancient warriors.

a ye ye ye ye ye ye ye
a yo yo yo yo yo yo yo
da a ye loom boom
da a ye loom boom

boom/boom
boom/boom

boom/boom
boom/boom
you. griot of the wind
glorifying red gums smiling tom-tom teeth.

MARCHERS HEADED FOR WASHINGTON, BALTIMORE, 1963

Remica L. Bingham

On Sunday—the amen-scent of fresh meat, apples
bearing nutmeg, collards simmered vinegar-sweet.

For days my father's mother let dawn rub
the back of her neck and shoulders, rising
in time to see the moon.

On Monday—fried chicken battered
with whole flour and double-A eggs,
seasoned with onion salt and lemon pepper.

As shards of light brightened
the darkest spot in her kitchen—the deep
slit that held last winter's preserves—she'd leave her work
and enter the bedroom her four sons shared.

On Tuesday—fresh Virginia ham, sliced thick,
sweetened with maple sap turned molasses.

Wiping at the sleep clouding their eyes,
one by one her boys marched
to the closet searching for the starched sets
of hand-me-down Sunday best awaiting them,

On Wednesday—pot roast and hotwater cornbread,
the cornmeal sifted as fine as loose road dust
lifting to settle on trousers and lace socks.

If all was right—each bowtie and collar
securely in place—she would line them up
in seats on the porch—even the youngest,
not yet five—then kneel, daily, offering
brief instructions: *Listen, children, and watch.*

On Thursday—smoked turkey, bronzed with heavy
brown sugar, stuffed with new potatoes and corn.

When the morning cooking was done and more
waited in pots atop the stove for the afternoon,
she began piling plates so high
they had to be doubled, covered in foil
and set in brown paper bags strong enough
to endure fifty more stone-ridden miles.

On Friday—fish and loaves, tanned backs of whiting
and yeast rolls passed from hand to hungry hand
until each passerby signaled enough.

When travelers approached, the first son
to spot them would stand and shout, *Here two come,
Mama*—or three or four, even nine came
into view once. Rushing to the door with arms
outstretched, he'd clutch the plates warming
his small hands, then go to the roadside with her message:

This is for the journey, my mama said,
in hopes that none of you will ever stop.

She fed hundreds that way, never seeing
any face close enough to recall it
clearly, her name unknown by those saying grace.
Her marching—from kitchen to porch, then
steadily back and back again—all but in place.

AND YEAH...THIS IS A LOVE POEM

Nikki Giovanni

(October 16, 1995)

It's not that I don't respect the brother in Baltimore or Washington or even some parts of Northern Virginia because I do   It's just that this is different

The brother who had to wake up before dawn, get into a car that may or may not need a new muffler, a new set of spark plugs, some attention to the motor but who decided none the less that "Yes" he had to heed the call to go to Washington DC   That's the brother I want to talk about

Not at all, please understand,   that I don't have a high regard for the brother who got on the bus   Getting on buses has always been a central revolutionary act of Black America   Just ask Plessy or Parks No   Getting on a bus is an act of responsibility   An act of bravery
An act of commitment to change

But the brother who rose from his warm bed   Who made his own coffee because his wife pretended to be asleep because she was scared that he might not come back alive and she didn't want to let him see her fear in her eyes 'cause she knew he needed to go even if he wouldn't come back alive That's the brother I want to talk about here

I want to talk about the young brother who just didn't understand why everything he did no matter how hard he tried never seemed to come out right How if he went bowling and got nine pins the 10th pin would just stand there mocking the ball heading for the gutter How if he bumped into someone on the street and said a simple "I'm sorry" somebody else would jump in his face but if he didn't say anything then someone said he was uncouth or how sometimes people would even deliberately run into him so he joined with other people like him and instead of calling it a Benevolent Society or a Brotherhood or something wonderful and romantic like Elks and Masons and Lions or Rotarians they called it a "Gang" indicating it was a "nest" of "vipers" and terms like that indicating things that we find dirty and unacceptable How when four or five white boys rape a mentally handicapped girl they are just exercising bad judgment but when four or five black boys rape a jogger they are all animals and this is not for any brother who rapes any female and it's not for anyone who hurts women or other vulnerable life forms but just a word or two about black boys who don't understand why everything they ever tried to do just never seems to turn out right and I think "Of course" "Yes" "Why wouldn't they cry themselves to sleep" when all that they want and want to be they already know is denied them Why wouldn't they be afraid of the dark Why wouldn't their hearts be broken when the people they love…mothers…fathers…aunts…uncles…girlfriends…good buddies… teachers…preachers…all turn out to be untrue And please don't tell me that basketball and baseball and football aren't the way to go that they should get their education when their education will only tell them to get a talent because the people who get up if not out of these cesspools we call the inner city have something more than a high school degree behind them and you have to be some kind of real fool to not see that they see who makes the money and who doesn't This is for the brother, however, who does, indeed, believe that there can be   should be   must be   a change

It's not that I am in any way unhappy about the brother who has a fine home, a car that is always serviced on time, a job with health benefits, a pretty wife, happy smart children, a dog that obeys. I'm proud and happy for him and his because I know a people cannot do better unless individuals do better but this is about the brother who stands on the street corners singing five part a cappela harmony and the brother who does break dancing under the street lights and the brothers who created rap because they took the music classes away so the brothers scratched then they invented CDs so the brothers rapped then they said Rap is the enemy of women as if Bob Dole and Rush Limbaugh and self satisfied Republicans with bumper sticker mentalities don't exist so this is for the brother who is simply trying to find a tone to soothe his soul while everyone wants to make him the reason America is way off track

And this is about the brother who knowing he is a better person than even he thinks he is got in his car in Detroit or Cincinnati or St. Louis and headed for Washington not knowing if he would be the only brother to show up for the Day of Atonement but knowing if he was the only brother then on this day at this time he would be the brother to stand and say to himself, his brothers and the folks whom he loves and who love him I Am Sorry That Things Are Not Different and that is a mighty powerful thing to say because people want to make you make miracles when all any of us can actually say is I Wish It Would Be Different but this is for the brother who was willing to be the only brother so that if there would be laughter as he stood alone on the Mall he still said I will stand because today it doesn't matter if I am alone I need to stand and testify and yeah this is a love poem for that brother who decided for this one point in time I will be my better self…And we all are very proud of you

THE CAROUSEL

Gloria C. Oden

"I turned from side to side, from image to image to put you down."
—Louise Bogan

An empty carousel in a deserted park
rides me round and round,
forth and back,
from end to beginning,
like the tail that drives the dog.

I cannot see:
sight focuses shadow where once
pleased scenery,
and in this whirl of space
only the indefinite is constant.

This is the way of grief:
spinning in the rhythm of memories
that will not let you up
or down,
but keeps you grinding through
a granite air.

ONLY EVERYTHING I OWN
Patricia Smith

This is my house.
This was my grandfather's house.
This is my thin wood, spidered pane.
These are my cobwebs, my four walls,
my silverfish, my bold roaches.
I bury my hands in that little garden,
cool them in the broken earth.
My food comes from my garden.
At my table, I slice the peppers,
seed the tomatoes, chop mint,
rip bitter green into wooden bowls.
The tiny pine table is my whole kitchen,
daddy's legacy, my certain warm nurture.
I dream loud in this house. I pull my bed
down from that wall, and I fall to my knees.
next to it to question this shelter.
I sleep while a limp breeze dies at the window,
waking to dawn tangled with my dust.
This is my house.
Let's step out into the steam,
sip new breath from a Mason jar,
find a sleeping rhythm for our chairs.
Let's wait patiently for the rain.
That blistered sky has learned my days
and hates me for everything I have. As it should.

LOT'S DAUGHTER DREAMS OF HER MOTHER

Opal Moore / TRACK 28 / READ BY ETHEL MORGAN SMITH

I
in my dream of roads
each turn glitters,
the road remembers your footsteps.
each night is a crossroad
and I must choose
a babylon burning and be cursed,
or reason.
mother, this choosing is hard—

these roads all slip away from me,
smooth and white.
in the moon light the dust shines
my feet are white with dust
and light.
what would you wish for me?
would you wish me Sodom? or safety?
which sacrifice?

mother your body is a road stretching back,
your memory intersects the spine
where I stand with my white feet
upon your heart,

you are my road
you are my cross and crossing,
you are my reaching back
and my intention,

you are my genesis my bedlam
you are my beginnings,
you are my death
in full stride

II
what if I came upon you in the road
sealed in the gray ash of your indecision
abandoned by angels
death caught
in full stride
like walking liberty.
your torch
is what you left behind:
the crime of knowing your place
the places you knew
secret couplings birthing blankets
a baby's sloppy open smile
first pains of blood sex betrayals
broken feathers,
knowing what is human—

III
you turned
looked back, they say.
they cannot say what you saw.

IV
I am your daughter
I lie down beside your husband
My flesh turns to water and salt
in his dreams he murmurs of angels

V
you and I
are women not angels
and practical.
in darkness I throw out my hands
wait for the dark to open
in darkness I kiss your fathomless face
taste your thirsty tears
in my dream
your shiny footprints shame me
50 tell me
tell me
what glimpse of future
turned you back?

I am your silence
your cross your road—
is this sleep?

VI
mother, oh! Mother—
I am turning—
my road is feathers.

THE GIRLFRIEND'S TRAIN
Nikky Finney

"You write like a Black woman who's never been hit
before."

I read poetry in Philly
for the first time ever.
She started walking up,
all the way, from in back
of the room.

From against the wall
she came,
big coat, boots,
eyes soft as candles
in two storms blowing.

Something she could not see
from way back there but
could clearly hear in my voice,
something she needed to know
before pouring herself back out
into the icy city night.

She came close to get a good look,
to ask me something she found
in a strange way missing
from my Black woman poetry.

Sidestepping the crowd
ignoring the book signing line,
she stood there waiting
for everyone to go, waiting
like some kind of Representative.

And when it was just the two of us
she stepped into the shoes of her words:

Hey,
    You write real soft.
    Spell it out kind.
    No bullet holes,
    No open wounds,
    In your words.
    How you do that?
    Write like you never been hit before?

But I could hardly speak,
all my breath held ransom
by her question.

I looked at her and knew:
There was a train on pause somewhere,
maybe just outside the back door
where she had stood, listening.

A train with boxcars
that she was escorting somewhere,
when she heard about the reading.

A train with boxcars
carrying broken women's bodies,
their carved up legs and bullet riddled
stomachs momentarily on pause
from moving cross country.

Women's bodies;
brown, black and blue,
laying right where coal, cars,
and cattle usually do.

She needed my answer
for herself and for them too.
Hey,
      We were just wondering
      how you made it through
      and we didn't?

I shook my head.
I had never thought about
having never been hit
and what it might have
made me sound like.

      You know how many times I been stabbed?

She raised her blouse
all the way above her breasts,
the cuts on her resembling
some kind of grotesque wallpaper.

How many women are there like you?

Then I knew for sure.

She had been sent in from the Philly cold,
by the others on the train,
to listen, stand up close,
to make me out as best she could.

She put my hand overtop hers
asked could we stand up
straight back to straight back,
measure out our differences
right then and there.

She gathered it all up,
wrote down the things she could,
remembering the rest to the trainload
of us waiting out back for answers.
Full to the brim with every age
of woman, every neighborhood
of woman, whose name
had already been forgotten.

The train blew its whistle,
she started to hurry.

I moved towards her
and we stood back to back,
her hand grazing the top
of our heads,
my hand measuring out
our same widths,
each of us recognizing
the brown woman latitudes,
the Black woman longitudes
in the other.

I turned around
held up my shirt
and brought my smooth belly
into her scarred one;
our navels pressing,
marking out some kind of new
equatorial line.

BACK FROM THE ARMS OF BIG MAMA
Afaa Michael Weaver

an avuncular song for Alya Amani McNeill

In this room, in this chamber,
the sun stands like a woman
in an old cotton dress in August
shelling peas under maple shade.
In this room your great-grandmother,
Big Mama, slept away under the eyes
of the council of her daughters,
who kept a vigil, a deathwatch,
rocking back and forth in their chairs,
humming unexpected hymns,
huddling close together, making room
for the angels, seven feet tall
in blue pinstripe suits with silver
lights for eyes. Your great aunts waited
in this room where my mother
watched the door in the firmament
as these angels walked away with Big Mama.
Here my mother agreed to die.
And here I hold your entire body,
one month into the world,
brought here by my baby sister.
I show an old rough face
that has laughed and cried
with lips that want to pucker
against your candy cheeks.
I feel like a giant

suddenly discovering in his hands
the delicate and splendiferous
fragrance of the first breaths
ever taken by a tiny life,
my hands that have struck,
my hands that have caressed,
my hands that have pulled
against the hem of heaven.
I want to give all,
all that I own and may earn
so that you might have peace,
give all like St. Francis of Assisi
to lessen the pain and tears,
to make you go into the cavern
of this corpulent world
like Sojourner Truth, name
blazing against greed and lies.
I tell you your destiny
for which I am accountable,
tell you how you will grow
and shine brilliant among women,
attend Ivy League universities,
become a doctor when I am old
and desperately in need of one,
how you will not take
any of the shit men give to women,
how you will prosper and know
very little pain as now
the host of thousands
of minute soprano angels
who minister to the newborn

are here chanting a song
for children, something unpretentious
and familiar, like nothing I know.
Each time one of them
leans over to your beautiful ear
and says softly, invisibly,
"Alya, you are home, child,"
you smile and stretch and coo
in the arms of a big old uncle
with a scarred life who has come
through the spirit's wars
still hungry for your wise eyes
stepping forward from the light.

MAMA'S PROMISE

Marilyn Nelson / TRACK 29 / READ BY THE POET

I have no answer to the blank inequity
of a four-year-old dying of cancer.
I saw her on TV and wept
with my mouth full of meatloaf.

I constantly flash on disasters now;
red lights shout *Warning. Danger.*
everywhere I look.
I buckle him in, but what if a car
with a grille like a sharkbite
roared up out of the road?
I feed him square meals,
but what if the fist of his heart
should simply fall open?
I carried him safely
as long as I could,
but now he's a runaway
on the dangerous highway.
Warning. Danger.
I've started to pray.

But the dangerous highway
curves through blue evenings
when I hold his yielding hand
and snip his minuscule nails
with my vicious-looking scissors.
I carry him around
like an egg in a spoon,
and I remember a porcelain fawn,
a best friend's trust,
my broken faith in myself.
It's not my grace that keeps me erect
as the sidewalk clatters downhill
under my rollerskate wheels.

Sometimes I lie awake
troubled by this thought:
It's not so simple to give a child birth;
you also have to give it death,
the jealous fairy's christening gift.

I've always pictured my own death
as a closed door,
a black room,
a breathless leap from the mountaintop
with time to throw out my arms, lift my head,
and see, in the instant my heart stops,
a whole galaxy of blue.
I imagined I'd forget,
in the cessation of feeling,
while the guilt of my lifetime floated away
like a nylon nightgown,
and that I'd fall into clean, fresh forgiveness.

Ah, but the death I've given away
is more mine than the one I've kept:
from my hands the poisoned apple,
from my bow the mistletoe dart.

Then I think of Mama,
her bountiful breasts.
When I was a child, I really swear,
Mama's kisses could heal.
I remember her promise,
and whisper it over my sweet son's sleep:

> *When you float to the bottom, child,*
> *like a mote down a sunbeam,*
> *you'll see me from a trillion miles away:*
> *my eyes looking up to you,*
> *my arms outstretched for you like night.*

BOP: A WHISTLING WOMAN
Lyrae Van Clief-Stefanon

Mama couldn't break me
of whistling like a boy the way she
stopped me hollering across streets
at boys I knew. *Let them recognize you.*
Young ladies don't raise their voices.
She knew or thought she knew
somewhere inside her, I
would not end well.

A whistling woman and a crowing hen
always come to no good end.

Let some boy use you if you want!
Her imperatives ran together. She glared,
tight-lipped at the threat of my summer days spent less
tight-legged, her fear, so ardent,
of one wrong wind, vibrating high-pitched,
passing between my lips.

A whistling woman and a crowing hen
always come to no good end.

This morning, train and teakettle catch the devil,
fifteen finches outside my kitchen window—
whose lessons do I choose?
Seven years without a slip
beneath my skirts. I'll flirt
with destruction, shame my kin.

A whistling woman and a crowing hen
always come to no good end.

HOMAGE TO MY HIPS

Lucille Clifton / TRACK 30 / READ BY ENNIS McCRERY

these hips are big hips.
they need space to
move around in.
they don't fit into little
petty places. these hips
are free hips.
they don't like to be held back.
these hips have never been enslaved,
they go where they want to go
they do what they want to do.
these hips are mighty hips.
these hips are magic hips.
I have known them
to put a spell on a man and
spin him like a top!

TRAIN RIDE
Kwame Dawes

Hard to picture those sweet boys
nameless black boys in the gut

of a slow moving freight train
crawling towards a new place.

Hard to see them take turns
on the pinkness of those white girls,

Still, I see the faces of those two
smiling on the bright newsprint,

making strong men wince
at the thought of this travesty,

their indulgent day-dreams
of rocking to some decadent beat

of the train, nine ejaculations,
nine fallen selves, howling, howling.

Don't have a mind for names,
but I learnt the names of the two:

Ruby Bean and Victoria Price,
like icons of a time past,

heard them carry like songs
in that hall there on 155th Street

and Rockland Palace, where we gathered
to pray for them Scottsboro boys,

to pray for their souls, forgiveness for
their dumb sin of watching those girls

with fiddling and more on their minds,
with the taste of taboo salivating their mouths.

Victoria Price and Ruby Dean.
I strengthen the pure resolve of my ways,

the intact hymen of my twenty-year-old womb,
not loose and wayward like those crazy two.

We cherish the dignity of our righteousness
gleaming white beside the white girls' sin.

No tears for the children, tears are hard
to come by when you've seen boys gathered

and whipped and worse for looking too hard,
for thinking of touching, for even smelling

and turning away from the breeze left behind
by white young girls like those two.

All you feel to say is old people's wisdom:
"You make your bed, you lay in it. You know better."

Can't believe those Scottsboro boys
had no idea what history they was messing with

rocking on that old freight train,
cutting through the heart of America.

TRAIN RIDES
Nikki Giovanni / TRACK 31 / READ BY VIRGINIA C. FOWLER

for William Adkins and Darrell Lamont Bailey

so on the first day of fall only not really because it's still early October you
sort of get the feeling that if you wear that linen blouse with that white suit
one more time someone from the fashion police will come and put some sort
of straitjacket on you or even worse CNN *Hard Copy Politically Incorrect* will
come film you and there you will be shamed before the world caught in the
wrong material after the right season has passed and though you have long
ago concluded that jail might make sense for folk who drink and drive and
jail certainly makes sense for folk who beat their wives and children and
there could be a good case that jail would be significant to folk who write
bad checks or don't pay their bills you know for a fact not just in your
heart that there is no excuse for prison unless you just want to acknowledge
that building anything at all is good for the economy but if that is the
case why spend the money on building prisons when a region a state a
community won't spend the money on building houses schools recreation
centers retirement complexes hospitals and for that matter shelters for hurt
neglected and abused animals so it's not just the building but actually what
is being built though you can't always tell that from watching roads go up
since roads always take so long to build by the time they are built they are
obsolete and we could have had a wonderful rail system if we hadn't been
more interested in Ferguson winning instead of Plessy and the entire system
collapsed under the weight of racism you are glad you do not go to jail but
rather are shamed or more accurately fear being shamed into proper dress
but on the first day of all when you know it's time to break down the deck
and put the flowerpots away since you could not actually afford to purchase

all-weather flowerpots and when you gave it a second thought you said to yourself I don't think I should throw this good soil away and you now in order to save money are on your way to Lowe's where you will purchase a big thing with a top that fits and stupid you you never even remembered that you can't possibly carry the soil down so in order to save the soil that you can't afford to replace you now have to hire two young men to carry the aforementioned soil-loaded thing with the tight top down the stairs to place it under the porch only your dog has been scratching and barking and moaning and you fear no really you know that little mother mouse is back and last year it was quite a dilemma and the dog kept seeing these little nuts and of course those mouse droppings and you were actually going to kill her but your nose was running so you went to the tissue box and the tissue was all chewed up so you lifted the box and there clearly was something in it and to be very honest you were scared because no matter what we say human beings don't do well with other life-forms but something made you peer down into the box and there were two bright eyes looking back and you really expected her to run only she didn't and then you realized it was because of the babies which you more sensed than saw and even though you have to admit to yourself you are afraid you take the box and place it in a hollow log in the meadow because even though you are a mother and understand why she did not run because you wouldn't have left your baby you know that you cannot live with mother mouse though of course now that you have paid to put the soil under the porch you understand you have put a sign out: MICE WELCOME

and this poem recognizes that

so when you find yourself on the first day of fall which is not actually
the first day but simply early October and because it has been such a
dry hot summer the leaves aren't really turning so it looks enough like
late spring to make you think back to when you and your sister used to
catch the train from Cincinnati to Knoxville to go spend the summer with
your grandparents and you thought you were pretty well grown because
Mommy didn't have to travel with you and the two of you were given
money which is not exactly true because your sister was given money and
you were told to ask her if you wanted something and we couldn't wait
to get to Jellico because the man came on the train with ham sandwiches
which were made with butter instead of mayonnaise and ice cold little
Cokes in a bottle and we had enough for that though we always shared the
potato chips and we didn't have a care that the world was not a warm and
welcoming place but we didn't realize that all up and down the line there
was a congregation of Black men looking out for us that no one said or did
anything to disturb our sense of well-being and what a loss that more Black
men are in prison than on trains which don't exist protecting two little girls
from the horrors of this world allowing them to grow up thinking people
are kind so even though we lived in a segregated world and even though
everybody knows that was wrong that band of brothers put their arms
around us and got us from our mother to our grandmother seamlessly

and this poem recognizes that

and I do have a lawn jockey next to the river birch just a bit to the back of the birdbaths besides the bleached cow's head the ceramic elephant the rabbit and the talking dogs and you can easily see that I collect foolish things but they make me happy and I was ecstatic to see *Emerge* put Clarence Thomas the poster boy for lawn jockeys on the cover because I agree with the folk who say give Scalia two votes and save a salary since Thomas must surely be causing Thurgood Marshall many a turn-over in his grave while he talks about the disservice done to him by affirmative action though old Clarence didn't sell hurt until the nazi right was buying and I really don't understand how some people can take advantage of every affirmative initiative from college to law school to EEOC to the Supreme Court and say these programs do not work and even old foolish Shelby Steele was saying his children didn't need a scholarship as if the existence of the scholarship should be eliminated since he didn't and what kind of sense is that when you take a pitiful little dumbbunny like Armstrong Williams who says things like my parents taught me to work hard and behave myself as if other parents gave lessons: *Now, Kwame, I want you to practice laziness today. You were far too busy yesterday* or worse: *Now, Kieshah, I expect loose morals from you. All last week you was studying and cleaning the house and helping out at the church and visiting the sick in the hospital and we just can't have none of that* and that is why those little lawn jockeys for the right are so despicable because they lack not only good sense but common compassion and like the old jokes about Black people being just like a bunch of crabs the Black right is pulling people down because they think if they don't knock Black people down they will not be able to stay where they are and they are of course right because the only usefulness they have is to stand in opposition to progress

and this poem recognizes that

so your back hurts anyway but you have to close things down as winter
will be here and no matter what else is wrong with winter the little lawn
jockeys will get covered the mice find a home and little girls travel back
and forth with the love of Black men protecting them from the cold and
even when the Black men can't protect them they wish they could which
has to be respected since it's the best they can do and somehow you want
to pop popcorn and make pig feet and fried chicken and blueberry muffins
and some sort of baked apple and you will sit near your fire and tell tales of
growing up in segregated America and the tales will be so loving even the
white people will feel short-changed by being privileged and we call it the
blues with rhythm and they want it to be rock and roll and all the thump
thump thump coming from cars is not Black boys listening to rap but all
boys wishing they could be that beautiful boy who was a seed planted in
stone who grew to witness to the truth and who always kept it real and lots
of times there is nothing we can do through our pain and through our tears
but continue to love

and this poem recognizes that

A GREAT GRANDDADDY SPEAKS
Lamont B. Steptoe

For Edward Dawon, Sr.

"Boy,
you tell my tale 'cause
I couldn't read
couldn't write
back there in slavery's night
worked from 'can't see to can't see'
I wasn't born free!
Somehow, in my blood
I knew you'd come along
pick up the pieces
make a song!"

EDDIE PRIEST'S BARBERSHOP & NOTARY

Kevin Young

Closed Mondays

is music is   *men*
off early from work   is waiting
for the chance at the chair
while the eagle claws holes
in your pockets   keeping
time   by the turning
of rusty fans   steel flowers with
cold breezes   is having nothing
better to do   than guess at the years
of hair   matted beneath the soiled caps
of drunks   the pain of running
a fisted comb through stubborn
knots   is the dark dirty low
down blues   the tender heads
of sons fresh from cornrows   all
wonder at losing   half their height
is a mother gathering hair   for good
luck   for a soft wig   is the round

difficulty of ears   the peach
faced boys asking Eddie
to cut in parts and arrows
wanting to have their names read
for just a few days   and among thin
jazz   is the quick brush of a done
head   the black flood around
your feet   grandfathers
stopping their games of ivory
dominoes   just before they read the bone
yard   is winking widowers announcing
cut it clean off   I'm through courting
and hair only gets in the way   is the final
spin of the chair   a reflection of
a reflection   that sting of wintergreen
tonic   on the neck of a sleeping snow
haired man   when you realize it is
your turn   you are next

VIEW OF THE LIBRARY OF CONGRESS FROM PAUL LAURENCE DUNBAR HIGH SCHOOL

Thomas Sayers Ellis

For Doris Craig and Michael Olshausen

A white substitute teacher
At an all-Black public high school,
He sought me out saying my poems
Showed promise, range, a gift,
And had I ever heard of T. S. Eliot?
No. Then Robert Hayden perhaps?

Hayden, a former colleague,
Had recently died, and the obituary
He handed me had already begun
Its journey home—from the printed page
Back to tree, gray becoming
Yellow, flower, dirt.

No river, we skipped rocks
On the horizon, above Ground Zero,
From the roof of the Gibson Plaza Apartments.
We'd aim, then shout the names
Of the museums, famous monuments,
And government buildings

Where our grandparents, parents,
Aunts, and uncles worked. Dangerous duds.

The bombs we dropped always fell short,
Missing their mark. No one, not even
Carlton Green who had lived in
As many neighborhoods as me,

Knew in which direction
To launch when I lifted Hayden's
Place of employment—
The Library of Congress—
From the obituary, now folded
In my back pocket, a creased map.

We went home, asked our mothers,
But they didn't know. Richard's came
Close: Somewhere near Congress,
On Capitol Hill, take the 30 bus,
Get off before it reaches Anacostia,
Don't cross the bridge into Southeast.

The next day in school
I looked it up—the National Library
Of the United States in Washington, D.C.
Founded in 1800, open to all taxpayers
And citizens. *Snap!* My Aunt Doris
Works there, has for years.

Once, on her day off, she
Took me shopping and bought
The dress shoes of my choice.
Loafers. They were dark red,
Almost purple, bruised—the color
Of blood before oxygen reaches it.

I was beginning to think
Like a poet, so in my mind
Hayden's dying and my loafers
Were connected, but years apart,
As was Dunbar to other institutions—
Ones I could see, ones I could not.

DRAPERY FACTORY, GULFPORT, MISSISSIPPI, 1956

Natasha Trethewey / TRACK 32 / READ BY JOANNE V. GABBIN

She made the trip daily, though
later she would not remember
how far to tell the grandchildren—
Better that way.
She could keep those miles
a secret, and her black face
and black hands, and the pink bottoms
of her black feet
a minor inconvenience.

She does remember thc mcn
she worked for, and that often
she sat side by side
with white women, all of them
bent over, pushing into the hum
of the machines, their right calves
tensed against the pedals.

Her lips tighten speaking
of quitting time when
the colored women filed out slowly
to have their purses checked,
the insides laid open and exposed
by the boss's hand.

But then she laughs
when she recalls the soiled Kotex
she saved, stuffed into a bag
in her purse, and Adam's look
on one white man's face, his hand
deep in knowledge.

SOME KIND OF CRAZY
Major Jackson

It doesn't matter if you can't see
Steve's 1985 CORVETTE: Turquoise-colored,
Plush purple seats, gold-trimmed
Rims that make little stars in your eyes

As if the sun is kneeling
At the edge of sanity. Like a Baptist
Preacher stroking the dark underside
Of God's wet tongue, he can make you

Believe. It's there, his scuffed wing-
Tips, ragged as a mop, shuffling
Concrete, could be ten-inch FIRESTONE
Wheels, his vocal chords fake

An eight cylinder engine that wags
Like a dog's tail as he shifts gears. Imagine
Steve moonstruck, cool, turning right
Onto RIDGE AVENUE, arms forming

Arcs, his hands a set of stiff *C's*
Overthrowing each other's rule,
His lithe body and head snap back
Pushing a stick-shift into fourth

Whizzing past UNCLE SAM'S PAWN
SHOP, past CHUNG PHAT'S STOP & GO.
Only he knows his destination,
His limits. Can you see him? Imagine

Steve, moonstruck, cool, parallel,
Parking between a PACER and a PINTO—
Obviously the most hip—backing up,
Head over right shoulder, one hand

Spinning as if polishing a dream;
And there's Tina, wanting to know
What makes a man tick, wanting
A one-way trip to the stars.

We, the faithful, never call
Him crazy, crack-brained, just a little
Touched. It's all he ever wants:
A car, a girl, a community of believers.

FROM
A. Van Jordan

from ➤ prep. 1. Starting at (a particular place or time): As in, John was *from* Chicago, but he played guitar straight *from* the Delta; he wore a blue suit *from* Robert Hall's; his hair smelled like coconut; his breath, like mint and bourbon; his hands felt like they were *from* slave times when he touched me—hungry, stealthy, trembling. 2. Out of: He pulled a knot of bills *from* his pocket, paid the man and we went upstairs. 3. Not near to or in contact with: He smoked the weed, but, surprisingly, he kept it *from* me. He said it would make me too self-conscious, and he wanted those feelings as far away *from* us as possible; he said a good part of my beauty was that I wasn't conscious of my beauty. Isn't that funny? So we drank Bloody Mothers (Hennessey and tomato juice), which was hard to keep *from* him—he always did like to drink. 4. Out of the control or authority of: I was released *from* my mama's house, *from* dreams of hands holding me down, *from* the threat of hands not pulling me up, *from* the man that knew me, but of whom I did not know; released *from* the dimming of twilight, *from* the brightness of morning; *from* the love I thought had to look like love; *from* the love I thought had to taste like love, *from* the love I thought I had to love like love. 5. Out of the totality of:

I came *from* a family full of women; I came *from* a family full
of believers; I came *from* a pack of witches—I'm just waiting
to conjure my powers; I came *from* a legacy of lovers—I'm just
waiting to seduce my seducer; I came *from* a pride of proud
women, and we take good care of our young. 6. As being
other or another than: He couldn't tell me *from* his mother;
he couldn't tell me *from* his sister; he couldn't tell me *from*
the last woman he had before me, and why should he—we're
all the same woman. 7. With (some person, place, or thing)
as the instrument, maker, or source: Here's a note *from* my
mother, and you can take it as advice *from* me: A weak lover
is more dangerous than a strong enemy; if you're going to love
someone, make sure you know where they're coming *from*. 8.
Because of: Becoming an alcoholic, learning to walk away, being
a good speller, being good in bed, falling in love—they all come
from practice. 9. Outside or beyond the possibility of: In the
room, he kept me *from* leaving by keeping me curious; he kept
me *from* drowning by holding my breath in his mouth; yes,
he kept me *from* leaving till the next day when he said *Leave*.
Then, he couldn't keep me *from* coming back.

FREEDOM CANDY
E. Ethelbert Miller

So what kind of name is Omar?
I ask this new boy at school.
You named after a candy bar or what?
You know you too light to be milk chocolate

Omar looks at me and laughs.
Since that first smile he's my best friend,
maybe my best friend ever.

Folks call us the inseparables
like one of those old singing groups
my daddy is always talking about.

Omar is a muslim name Omar tells me.
I think it still sounds like a candy bar,
like O'Henry, Baby Ruth, Mars or Almond Joy.

Maybe his momma should have named him
Snickers because of the way he laughs.
Omar's name sounds like candy
and the way he acts is sweet to me.

Every teacher except Mrs. Greenfield thinks so.
Ms. Greenfield she don't like Muslims
and the rest of us she calls natural born sinners
because of the way we talk and behave.

Omar says we should tell Mrs. Greenfield
about herself since it's Black History Month.
So Omar stands up and says to Mrs. Greenfield:

How come you don't lead us somewhere?
Why you not like Harriet Tubman?
Why no field trips?
Why no trips to the museum or zoo?
Why we never go nowhere, why?

Mrs. Greenfield, she don't say nothing.
She just look at Omar as if he is the last Muslim
on earth and is about to die.

I think of how Omar says Muslims pray
five times a day and how cats have nine lives and
just maybe Omar might make it to 3 o'clock
or maybe he won't.

Suddenly Mrs. Greenfield has one of those
fainting spells just like old Moses Tubman.
She has to sit down behind her desk so
she tells me to go get her some water.

I feel free as I race down the hall
wondering how Omar can be sweet sometimes
and get on everyone's nerves the next.

My daddy once told me M&Ms
melt in your mouth and your hands
especially if you colored.

Wait until I tell Omar.

THE SUPREMES
Cornelius Eady

We were born to be gray. We went to school,
Sat in rows, ate white bread,
Looked at the floor a lot. In the back
Of our small heads

A long scream. We did what we could,
And all we could do was
Turn on each other. How the fat kids suffered!
Not even being jolly could save them.

And then there were the anal retentive,
The terrified brown-noses, the desperately
Athletic or popular. This, of course,
Was training. At home

Our parents shook their heads and waited.
We learned of the industrial revolution,
The sectioning of the clock into pie slices.
We drank cokes and twiddled our thumbs. In the
Back of our minds

A long scream. We snapped butts in the showers,
Froze out shy girls on the dance floor,
Pinpointed flaws like radar.
Slowly we understood: this was to be the world.

We were born insurance salesmen and secretaries,
Housewives and short order cooks,
Stockroom boys and repairmen,
And it wouldn't be a bad life, they promised,
In a tone of voice that would force some of us
To reach in self-defense for wigs,
Lipstick,

Sequins.

Jazz Suite

NIKKI SAVE ME
Michele Scott

Teetering on the gray wall
Marigolds and pansies below
My body sways to "So What"
Not dance, but leans
    Passerby passing me by
  above my height
She says she doesn't know why the caged bird sings
My body sways to "So What"
Not dance, but leans
Nikki save me
Shiny suit man stops and gives me his hand
I
  f
      a
       l
        l
into the crack of the concrete
Dancing to the rhythm of "So What"

UNTITLED
Kwame Alexander / TRACK 33 / READ BY NOVELLA NELSON

Nikki, if you were a song
I'd call you jazz

Clap for you
Snap to you

Sing with you
Swing with you

I'd color you Ellington
Elegant

and Essential
in my life

HAIKU
DJ Renegade

Jazz is
the way brown sugar
would sound
if it was sprinkled
in your ear

UNTITLED
Nadir Lasana Bomani

i have been in debt
since birth when mama put the
phone bill in my name

UNTITLED
Leodis McCray

I wish I could've seen it
The burning buildings and crosses
That left charred bodies to burn the memories in deep
What must it have been like to feel the festering fear that never leaves you
  alone
To be so scared you had a reason to be courageous

The stage was set for revolution

I sigh just a little
Knowing that I'll never know the taste of whites only pies
Because the taste of liberty was placed on my lips at birth by my forefathers
  and fly mothers
They who knew the feel of the lash
Even when they were tilling the soil that would ensure that my roots ran
  deep

Even now I can hear the moans of black women held captive in ages long
  past
I should've been there to wipe away their tears
To show the world I have what it takes to be strong
After all
Once upon a time I would've been bred to be a warrior

I would have bled for my cause
To clear the fight out of my system
But now the battle is unclear

Not like in the days when you knew the bad guy would be wearing white
Either over his head or in their genetics
They were the ghosts who haunted you persistently

But not me
For the taunts that once were our welcome to the auction block
Are mere whispers of what they once were
Whispers on the howling winds that
Leave levees in shambles
Ripping homes and families to pieces

You knew a time when daddy was strange fruit because he didn't want his
    kids to grow
up in the world that he did
Now families are fatherless because morality's not enough to keep daddy
    from breaking the law
But when our babies are starving who can blame him
Because even though Jim Crow is dead
Uncle Sam is working overtime to keep the projects poor

And since we don't need plantations any longer
The slaves have outlived their usefulness
So we're fed their castaways in hopes that diabetes will bring the surgeons
    to take
Kunta's leg
They know we can't get a million men to march if we're hopping along
    behind them

Oh no
I'll never know the days of the black panthers
Because they send us to prisons to learn our lessons
Public school or penitentiary
The metal detectors make them feel the same to me
While guards and sub par teachers
Make violence our mode of expression

If we kill ourselves off young enough
Who's going to carry the legacy you left us

While the moans of African mothers slowly become the cries of drug
    addicted babies born in the ghettos
Slave ships are blowing in on the force of hurricanes
Rusted chains are melted down to make impenetrable bars
And on top of it all we still can't read

But I can write
And I'm angry
Time to set the stage for revolution

THAT AND SOME MO'
DJ Renegade

Ebonics is our lingo, yo can you get with this
It's a flatted fifth away, from Caucasian linguistics
It's english infused with African characteristics
Yeah, that and some mo' shit

See the Kalahari sun, softly fuels our smile
And our rhythm's flow forth funky like the Nile
Cuz ancestral spirits influence our style
That and some mo' shit

Check out the jelly, jam shake, as a hip flips wide
the candied yam brown sweetness, of a fly sister's stride
And the Nubian queenly class, she possess's inside
Yeah, that and some mo' shit

Feel the Djembe rumble, as a fleet foot flies
The warrior's defiance, a brother's step implies
and the ancient tribal wisdom, that's reflected in his eyes
That and some mo' shit.

See we've built knowledge of self, to put hate in check
So a new African is now in effect
We're centered and proud, and cold coming correct
Yeah, that and some mo' shit.

SOMETIME IN THE SUMMER THERE'S OCTOBER

Tony Medina

for Staci

though it's summer
i'm thinking of fall,
thinking of fall,
walking in the rain
on my way to you

I

I always liked the fall
walking down the street
in gray light afternoon
the leaves rising up off the curb
falling through the trees
a sunny somber Coltrane melody
rocking back and forth inside my skull

I always liked the way you smiled
sipping hot tea
in warm empty cafes,
windows clouded wet
with the memories
of your poetry

II

in the hospital room
your blinds are shut
so the light won't eat
into your bones

you lie in your bed
folded hairless
in a puddle
of dead skin

your sheets are soaked
in sweat
your pillow full of snot
and tears

and though they carve you up
into a jigsaw puzzle
of your former self
you refuse to sew yourself up
from the world

III

you smile at me
as I clown for you
as I clown for me
unable to swallow
this image of you

IV

what impostors we are:
you in that broken skin
trying to hold your bones
together in its web
of dust and blood

and me trying
to keep
from sobbing
like the night
my grandmother died
in her light blue robe

V

you try to talk,
your smock dangling
off your bones
as your laughter shifts
the light in the room,
the blinds masticating
the sun, and you
forcing out a smile
through the impostor
that traps your soul,
in my eye's spying
examination
of what is now you
there is still
the you
i remember

with quick bright eyes
and attitude
the lips I've touched
the toes my tongue remembers,
that one sunny Sunday
in blue socks
that curled
as we baptized each other
in poetry,
the music
the wooden floor made
against your skin

(how I wanted
to keep you
in *that* light)

VI

but here, now,
you are in a dark cell
on death row,
a political prisoner
in Life's endless Kafkaesque
nightmare
always absurd and unfair,
playing Russian roulette
with your sanity,
your sense of reality

Death, the final judge
and jury
Death, the governing body
with the power
to absolve
and release
and heal

and Cancer,
the prosecuting attorney,
trying to exhaust you
of your appeals
to live
leaving you with no other option
but to put yourself
in the hands
of bone marrow transplants
and corporate science
and other people's
blood

and though my days
are not as uncertain
as yours
if i could i would
will you them

DANCING NAKED ON THE FLOOR
Kwame Alexander

write a poem with tension...like some baptist church
split...let it walk a tightrope...between congregation
one and congregation two...write a poem that finishes
school...a magna cum laude poem...let it be momentous...
learn something meaningful...share something significant...
write a poem that looks good...A Billie Holiday poem...
not homely or sway-backed...give it posture, poise and
profile...turn our heads when it walks by...stomp our feet
when it smiles...on some superficial level...make us want
to marry it or...at least remember its name the next
morning...write a poem that works...write a poem that
works...has a job and does it...promptly...follows rules and
responsibilities...gets a raise or at least a head nod...and
when it's not feeling well...give it sense enough to call in
sick...and not waste our time with unmet expectations...
write a poem that has a family...not some single life of
soiled one-night stands...I mean your poem should be
in a serious relationship...let it commit to something...
move beyond soap opera sex...let it be passionate...about
something...and if it gets excited...if it just has to get
physical...let it be in the privacy of its own beautiful
mind...cause we can watch cable at home...write a poem
that travels...gets outside of your cramped apartment...

leaves all that tired baggage…and catches a plane
somewhere…takes us on a journey fueled by imagination
and study…not television and film…one that has been
somewhere we haven't…write a poem that reads…
please…write…a…poem…that…reads…more than
headlines and sitcom credits…a cultured poem…
…writes a poem that knows how to talk…not some
misbehaving foul-mouth looking for attention…an
eloquent poem…write a poem that dances…wild
and free…a gutsy poem…write a poem that cooks…
I mean it ain't got to bake a cake…but at least know
the ingredients…write a poem that exercises…cycling
is not required…but steps never hurt nobody…write a
poem that runs for office…it ain't got to win…but at
least campaign…get a clue poets…write a poem with
an inkling of suspicion…I mean it ain't got to solve a
crime…but let it at least offer us a tip…write a poem
that is contagious…write a poem that is contagious…
write a poem that is contagious…let it inspire…make
us…want to write a poem…about how brilliant…and
breathtaking…and tragic…and hopeful…life is

HARRIET TUBMAN'S EMAIL 2 MASTER
Truth Thomas

>Subject: directions to the new place

go
down past glass
ground in your salt shaker

make a right
between
arsenic sweet tea swallows

i am easy to find.
just take the fork where

mothers kill their babies
to keep them safe from you

and
look for
windows growing shotguns.

A RIVER THAT FLOWS FOREVER
Tupac Shakur / TRACK 34 / READ BY NOVELLA NELSON

4 Mother

As long as some suffer
      The River Flows Forever
As long as there is pain
      The River Flows Forever
As strong as a smile can be
      The River will Flow Forever
And as long as u R with me
      we'll ride the River Together

THE ROSE THAT GREW FROM CONCRETE
Tupac Shakur / TRACK 34 / READ BY NOVELLA NELSON

Did u hear about the rose that grew from a crack
in the concrete
Proving nature's laws wrong it learned 2 walk
without having feet
Funny it seems but by keeping its dreams
it learned 2 breathe fresh air
Long live the rose that grew from concrete
when no one else even cared!

ROCHELLE

Reuben Jackson

i want to have
an affair
with your
poems.

take the haiku you read
on a late night
plane to chicago,

sip bourbon
with that villanelle
in a penthouse
on central park
west.

or considering
your love for this city,

an apartment above
washington
harbor.

sky dimming
like a chandelier
at twilight,

slow kisses
for each word.

ALL THEIR STANZAS LOOK ALIKE
Thomas Sayers Ellis

All their fences
  All their prisons
All their exercises
  All their agendas
All their stanzas look alike
  All their metaphors
All their bookstores
  All their plantations
All their assassinations
  All their stanzas look alike
All their rejection letters
  All their letters to the editor
All their arts and letters
  All their letters of recommendation
All their stanzas look alike
  All their sexy coverage
All their literary journals
  All their car commercials
All their bribe-spiked blurbs
  All their stanzas look alike
All their favorite writers
  All their writing programs
All their visiting writers
  All their writers-in-residence
All their stanzas look alike
  All their third worlds

All their world series
  All their serial killers
All their killing fields
  All their stanzas look alike
All their state grants
  All their tenure tracks
All their artist colonies
  All their core faculties
All their stanzas look alike
  All their Selected Collecteds
All their Oxford Nortons
  All their Academy Societies
All their Oprah Vendlers
  All their stanzas look alike
All their haloed holocausts
  All their coy hetero couplets
All their hollow haloed causes
  All their tone-deaf tercets
All their stanzas look alike
  All their tables of contents
All their Poet Laureates
  All their Ku Klux classics
All their Supreme Court justices
  Except one, except one
Exceptional one. Exceptional or not,
  One is not enough.
All their stanzas look alike.
  Even this, after publication,
Might look alike. Disproves
  My stereo types.

FROM THE CENTER 2 THE EDGE
Asha Bandele

brother
if i had the time
& u had the inclination
i would wrap my tongue
around yr/tears
swallow them   taste u
in places u had traded away
i'd reclaim them 4 u
love u back thru the years   back
into yr/gawky long-armed teenaged days   back
into yr/boyhood   into
yr/mother's belly
if that's where it started
i'd let u be born again
into the promise of
a world that does not grieve its color
i'd liquefy yr/pain
throw it past the wind
let my eyes be a mirror

u see yr/self in
& u would see yr/self
like I see u: a wide eyed would-be prophet of the urban nite
sketching fancy dreams
on cheap paper

yr/words are tricks
new-age illusions
i might have believed
but dead birds fell out yr/mouth
when u tried to talk
& I knew…

THE SUBTLE ART OF BREATHING
Asha Bandele

in the middle of everything i'm not doing   my doorbell rings it's the
landlady's lost son   i point him up the stairs mildly annoyed to have
been interrupted from my intent viewing of a soap opera   *one life to
live* ironic   now that i think about it

nobody ever suspects women like me poets politically conscious   watch
soap operas but we do   at least i do grateful   to retreat into the
fictitious chaos of somebody else's life

but this is not a poem about soap operas

it's just that i cannot find another way to begin   i mean how   would
you do it?

would you start with a father's scream lancing the air
with the little sister's indelicate weep.
or the acidic gurgle of a stomach in self-destructing
maybe you would simply begin like a broadcast journalist scanning a
teleprompter:

*in anchorage today a 30-year-old black woman was found in her apartment
dead of an overdose. The incident has been ruled a suicide…*

but this is not a poem about how to begin a poem
or a poem about lost sons and landladies
this is not a poem about soap operas

in islam they say from Allah we come to Allah we return leaving   the
curious among us hungry   for the story in between arrival and
departure   the person in the center   the thin arms desperate   to
stop the steady crush of closing walls   her first wall was daughter her
second was wife   not much room there to just be a woman
holy or unholy

but this is not a poem about religion

there are people who have accused me of creating the various & sundry
crises in my life
there are people who have accused me of refusing joy & of blanketing the
sun   but then there are people who know as i know that even
as we laugh   we cannot ignore the wincing in our eyes   we are not
crazy or invested in sadness   sister was it that you knew there was no
space to be second best or needy in a country swallowing up the earth from
the inside out   they incinerate their own children here i have seen them
scraping   their own 8 year olds into garbage bags   or compactors
whatever's efficient &

it might be that this is a political poem

forgive me
i feel guilty borrowing your family's pain   you were not my daughter
not my sister   i never even met you   your name & troubles were a
footnote   at the end of a discussion on lovers and where to go for dinner
that night   i know this space of mourning is not mine to occupy but i
cannot leave   your life reads like the details of my life & i must
know why   you are dead   i am not   yet we both were 30

black female & fighting histories of drugs violence separation loss start stop
start stop again   we are a ritual of everyday blackwoman experience
stories repeated on sally & geraldo ricki lake & the news nothing unusual
suicide?

been there   done that &

maybe this is a poem about *déjà vu* or a poem about phyllis hyman or billie
holiday maybe this is a poem about my grandmother or your best friend from
back in the day   maybe this is a poem about you but it is definitely not a
poem about invented crises fictitious lives or retreating pretending lying
turning away or even praying

this is not a poem about soap operas

once i was told that i was more than all of my hurting added up together
if i had known you   i would have told you that too   girl there
was more to you than your violent marriage   more than the brown girl
you became crouching   beneath dining room table   more to you
than the baby you lost or the last time you or any one of us gave ourselves up
like unwilling virgins to   cocaine vodka tonics cheap wine newports
columbian gold   & beer when the money got tight   girl there was clear
skin beneath your bruises   muscle behind the split ribs   a raving
beauty beyond *his* broke up sight & screams of *bitch lemme tell you something*
you ain't shit nasty funky ass stupid ho   & did you ever see her   even
once & if i did & if i told you we were the same woman sisters maybe
twins   would you have been able to hear me

can i ask you something?

was this the first time you felt powerful? did you feel   finally some
control   did you say to yourself   can't be yanked out from under this
table   gotta hiding place that muthafucka won't never find me in   did
you think   at last   a truth no one will ignore   that the world will
believe you   now   i just remember feeling very calm
as i slid into pieces of the splintered wood of my dormroom floor all those years
ago   you know what would have happened if you had survived been
surprised by somebody coming back in after the 18th pill?   you would
have tried to fight them as they tried to make you walk   they would have
dragged you up & down the floors till the ambulance arrived someone
would have slapped you to keep you awake   whoever found you
might have read your journals   displayed your diaries   said they
just wanted to understand   at the hospital   if you arrived unconscious
they would have made you eat a black chalk substance   to induce
vomiting   you would have vomited   uncontrollably   in front of
you   they would have stirred through it picking out the pills for analysis
     there is no other way to say this   besides i told you

this is not a poem about soap operas but

this may be a poem that warns breathing is a difficult and subtle art   it
may be a poem to say simply   i understand sister   after 3 attempts
& 9 years past the last one   i understand girl & i think this is a poem
that wants to assert itself   i'm proud even glad that i'm a survivor   &
sometimes when i am quiet & sometimes when i am scared & sometimes
when i am reflective & sometimes when i am scared & sometimes
sometimes when i am watching soap operas   i say oneday   i'm
gonna be even more than a survivor   i'll be a celebrant inside myself a
party girl in my own soul   i'll take myself out to fancy restaurants
bring me roses then make love to myself & in the heat of passion call out my
own name (*asha, asha...*)   yes   i'm gonna marry myself   does
that sound crazy?

martin luther king said *we may not get there together/but we as a people...*
& what if i do girl? get there   & find myself dancing wild in a bright silk
dress & high-heeled shoes   will you come too   ok   not now
but your next time around   be your own sensual dance partner in
high-heeled shoes fine as hell girl   & so so so   fulla
life

SOUTHERN UNIVERSITY, 1962
Kevin Young

for my father

Let's see   first afros I saw   were on these girls from
                SNCC   they had dark
berets with FREEDOM NOW on them   that barely
                covered their helmets
of hair   they sang of the struggle   of the non violent
                demonstration   in town
that weekend   By Saturday it was raining like hell   me
                and Greene
we were home boys   from Opelousas High   we were
                trying to pour in
the last of the blue and white buses this black man in
                town   had let SNCC use
I had my arm in the door   trying to get on out of the
                rain   and so split my
fiveninetyfive raincoat   right down the side   I tossed it
                on the ground
and me and Greene got on just before the bus pulled
                away   When we got
outside campus   ten big beefy white guys   with red
                faces and silent yellow
slickers to their knees   blocked the bus and began
                pounding and pounding
on the door with billy clubs   they tore the door off
                and stormed on

dragging the driver off the bus   throwing him in the
                    trunk   they said there
wasn't gonna be no demonstration today   not here   but
            once their lights
disappeared   under all that water   someone said let's
                    go   so me and Greene
and everyone else got off the anchored bus   and
                    walked the four
miles to town   by our soaking selves   When we got to
                    McKays   the WHITES
ONLY five&dime   it was empty as a drum   they knew
                    we were coming
had locked up and gone home   the street was a
                    sea   of umbrellas
and soon as the wind came   which of course it
                    did   my threeninetyfive
umbrella blew in on itself   so I left it on the walk   a
                    broken black
bird   as we started to march towards the city
                    council   Greene's fiveninety
five cardboard shoes   began falling apart   we had
                    started to cross Main
Street   I could just see the top of the white marble
                    building   when about

six cop cars   came wailing out of nowhere   a dozen or
                    so plainclothesmen
jumped out   holding these cans of tear gas   they
                    said   don't even try
crossing this street   go home and stop making trouble
                    just then the light
changed   turning from red to green   we crossed
                    the men clubbed us
threw their tears at us   they took out our wallets
                    took everything we had
and left it on the sidewalk   with our streaming eyes   with the rain

POETRY SHOULD RIDE THE BUS
Ruth Forman

poetry should hopscotch in a polka dot dress
wheel cartwheels
n hold your hand
when you walk past the yellow crackhouse

poetry should wear bright red lipstick
n practice kisses in the mirror
for all the fine young men with fades
shootin craps around the corner

poetry should dress in fine plum linen suits
n not be so educated that it don't stop in
every now n then to sit on the porch
and talk about the coins and goins of the world

poetry should ride the bus
in a fat woman's Safeway bag
between the greens n chicken wings
to be served with tuesday's dinner

poetry should drop by a sweet potato pie
ask about the grandchildren
n sit through a whole photo album
on a orange plastic covered lazyboy with no place to go

poetry should sing red revolution love songs
that massage your scalp
and bring hope to your blood
when you think you're too old to fight

yeah
poetry should whisper electric blue magic
all the years of your life
never forgettin to look you in the soul
every one in a while
n smile

BLUES FOR SPRING
Colleen J. McElroy

it should happen
on a train a face
you see in passing

a glance a kiss
just for the asking
it should happen

in a room where tea   wail the mighty sax
is served in thin china   and your friend Gordon
cups and Mendelssohn   calls suddenly

or Brahms musical verse   from Costa Rica
sugars the air   out-of-the-blue and says
or perhaps it happens   do you remember? and you

in a bar where Dexter   recognize only the steel
Gordon and his crowd   blue of the northern sky
of hoarse laughter   forlorn as winter

                                       or a note welded thin
                                       to sorrow the horizon
                                       so clear so close

                                       so naked a love
                                       that should come
                                       should happen soon

THE BICYCLE WIZARD
Sharan Strange

for my grandfather

His yard was a grave for lost wheels and frames,
like the aftermath of some crash derby.
I loved to watch as he tinkered, hoped
in vain for one custom-built, but unclaimed.
He'd lay out parts in schematic array, then
match sprockets and gears, rig and oil chains,
bolt seats, and clean spokes—silent all the while.
Then came the slight smile as he stood each
reincarnation against the barn. Sometimes

he'd let my older brother borrow one,
and for a few hours, I relished the feel
of my hands gripping the wide handlebars
and my small body hoisted above the earth.
I straddled those oversized bikes
wanting to speed, to soar, as he did,
over the smooth road between our houses
where I couldn't go unless on errand, where
I might ride to its end and turn into the world.

But I bumped along in tight circles, spinning
over the rutted, bald ground of my backyard,
missing the pecan and gum ball trees by a hair,
skirting heaps of lumber, rusted motors, pipes,
a shedful of tools—my father's years of junk.
With feet grazing the pedals and crotch
against the crossbar, I kicked and careened
until, throwing myself off, I stopped.

BICYCLES
Nikki Giovanni

Midnight poems are bicycles
Taking us on safer journeys
Than jets
Quicker journeys
Than walking
But never as beautiful
A journey
As my back
Touching you under the quilt

Midnight poems
Sing a sweet song
Saying everything
Is all right

Everything
Is
Here for us
I reach out
To catch the laughter

The dog thinks
I need a kiss

Bicycles move
With the flow
Of the earth

Like a cloud
So quiet
In the October sky
Like licking ice cream
From a cone
Like knowing you
Will always
Be there

All day long I wait
For the sunset

The first star
The moon rise

I move
To a midnight
Poem
Called
You
Propping
Against
The dangers

A CLEAN SLATE

Fred D'Aguiar

For Grace Theriault-Mayfield

Each morning I worked up spit
Aimed at my slate and wiped
Shirt-tail from corner to corner

Each day was a clean start
Born again and born *big-so*
As grownups loved to say

The day before disappeared
Somewhere between
My saliva and Terylene shirt

The new day promised
Something hitherto not
Seen or guessed about

A cobweb not there
The previous twenty-four hours
That overnight dew reveals

'A' for aubergine
Known to us as *balanjay*
'B' for bat for playing cricket

Until I filled the slate
With slant text my left hand
Told my right-side brain was new

Coins on the sea pressed by light
This morning sky wiped of stars
Chalk off my shirt climbing sun

SONG THROUGH THE WALL
Akua Lezli Hope

you will not punish me
you will not split me in two
you will not knock on my doors
you will not tap on my wall
you will not enter
you will not exit
you will not park your car in my garage
you will not contain your missile in my silo
you will not conjugate me
you will not fiddle faddle or dally me
you will not find my treasure
you will not lick my pot
you will not fill my refrigerator
you will not butter my roll
you will not toast my bagel

you will not baste my chicken

you will not taste my manna or sip my nectar

you will not fry my egg or lick my bowl

you will not yin my yang, ting my tang, or sniff my yoni

you will not raise my dead my spirits or my hopes

you will not run your trains down my tracks or through

my tunnel

you will not rain on me, flood me, thunder me or lance

me with your lightning rod

you will not be a bee to my flower nor a bear to my honey

you will not move my mountain nor the earth under my feet

you will not look at me and smile with those seducer's eyes

nor will you speak to me with that steel-melting voice

you will not know my next move

you will not guess what I need

you will not you will not you willnot make me love you

A SEAT SAVED
Shana Yarborough

Nobody sits in that chair
'Cuz it's filled with pipe smoke
Hard peppermint candy
A toothpick
And a small shot of brandy

Nobody sits in that chair
'Cuz it's filled with war stories
And happy days
Lessons learned
And wise old ways

Nobody sits in that chair
'Cuz it's filled with an old spice smell
A heartfelt love
Humor
And a blessing from above

Nobody sits in that chair
'Cuz it's filled with "dentured" smiles
A winking eye
A poker hand
A soft goodbye

Nobody
Sits in that
Chair

Because

Gentle
Love is
Still Sitting
There

SUNDAY GREENS
Rita Dove

She wants to hear
wine pouring.
She wants to taste
change. She wants
pride to roar through
the kitchen till it shines
like straw, she wants

lean to replace
tradition. Ham knocks
in the pot, nothing
but bones, each
with its bracelet
of flesh.

The house stinks
like a zoo in summer,
while upstairs
her man sleeps on.
Robe slung over
her arm and
the cradled hymnal,

she pauses, remembers
her mother in a slip
lost in blues,
and those collards,
wild-eared,
singing.

THE UNTITLED SUPERHERO POEM
Tonya Maria Matthews

I have SUPERPOWERS
Yes. Yes, I do

Faster than lazy welfare house hoes
more powerful than non-voting Negroes
able to relate to unsuspecting White Folk in a single
conversation

I am SUPERWOMAN

By day…
mild-mannered exception to that rule
but once on city streets
I blend into urban blocks like that mailbox
13-year co-workers from the next cubicle
can't see me
INVISIBLE

TELEKINETIC
Now in my human form
can't so much as move a school board to buy school
books for school children
but after 6 o'clock
can move crowds of innocent old white ladies
across streets and down blocks at inhuman speeds
with a single glance

I am that BEAST

Though powers did not manifest until late in life
as a child: acceptable
afro-puffs: adorable   then
the MUTANT GENES kicked in
hips grew to SUPERHUMAN PROPORTIONS
butt enlarged to NATIONAL SECURITY THREAT
hair grew in so nappy   so nappy
(it was   SUPERNATURAL)
that's when arch rival African Pride
started producing perm.
But get this…

I am also SHAPE-SHIFTER

I can walk into a convenience store
6 foot 9 inches black as night bald as day
weigh in at whopping 497 pounds
then leave
and by the time the cops catch me
I am   5'4" light-skinned with Afro
weighing 93 pounds   wet

Out of my homeland
where I was just an ordinary princess
abilities grew beyond imagination
vowed to use SUPERHUMAN STRENGTHS
to save my adopted homeworld
from the horrors of
whatever
so they would love me like SUPERMAN
but instead
they treat me like   the WONDER TWINS

pointless
powerless
and wondering   why
they ever brought me on the show
in the first place.

MERCY KILLING

Remica L. Bingham / TRACK 35 / READ BY NOVELLA NELSON

At Big Ma's, I stood in the middle of each room,
careful not to lean on walls or too near closets,
afraid the vermin—now outnumbering
the hairs on her head—would find their way
to my purse or pockets.

When asked to go to her drawer for antacid, I hesitated
knowing I'd have to reach in amidst their dark scattering
to soothe her. *These are the sacrifices we make*
my mother said while on the floor at Big Ma's feet,
clipping her toenails, using a slipper
to smash roaches as they came.

My father hated the dirtiness of any place
yet knelt, in his finest charcoal suit, near the phone cord—
twisting its disconnected wires—
surely aware of the thick dust graying his elbows and knees.
Until he heard a dial-tone and Big Ma said
I can call now if I need you, he did not rise.

Hours later, in public with our private lives well-clothed,
when I saw the silvery-brown pest slip
from his pants cuff—remembering my parents' selflessness,
their hushed mercy—I used my sharp-tipped shoes
to make a sacrifice and killed it—quiet, swift—without mentioning
my fear and without his ever knowing.

IF YOU SAW A NEGRO LADY
June Jordan

If you saw a Negro lady
sitting on a Tuesday
near the whirl-sludge doors of
Horn & Hardart on the main drag
of downtown Brooklyn

solitary and conspicuous as plain
and neat as walls impossible to
fresco and you watched her self-
conscious features shape about
a Horn & Hardart teaspoon
with a pucker from a cartoon

she would not understand
with spine as straight and solid
as her years of bending over floors
allowed

skin cleared of interest by a ruthless
soap   nails square and yellowclean
from metal files

sitting in a forty-year-old flush
of solitude and prickling
from the new white cotton blouse
concealing nothing she had ever noticed
even when she bathed and never
hummed a bathtub tune nor knew one

If you saw her square
above the dirty
mopped-on antiseptic floors
before the rag-wiped table tops

little finger   broad and stiff
in heavy emulation of a cockney

mannerism

would you turn her treat
into surprise by
observing

happy birthday

EGO TRIPPING
(THERE MAY BE A REASON WHY)

Nikki Giovanni / TRACK 36 / READ BY THE POET

I was born in the congo
I walked to the fertile crescent and built
    the sphinx
I designed a pyramid so tough that a star
    that only glows every one hundred years falls
    into the center giving divine perfect light
I am bad

I sat on the throne
    drinking nectar with allah
I got hot and sent an ice age to europe
    to cool my thirst
My oldest daughter is nefertiti
    the tears from my birth pains
    created the nile
I am a beautiful woman

I gazed on the forest and burned
    out the sahara desert
    with a packet of goat's meat
    and a change of clothes
I crossed it in two hours
I am a gazelle so swift
    so swift you can't catch me

    For a birthday present when he was three
I gave my son hannibal an elephant
    He gave me rome for mother's day
My strength flows ever on

My son noah built new/ark and
I stood proudly at the helm
    as we sailed on a soft summer day
I turned myself into myself and was
    jesus
    men intone my loving name
    All praises All praises
I am the one who would save

I sowed diamonds in my back yard
My bowels deliver uranium
    the filings from my fingernails are
    semi-precious jewels
    On a trip north
I caught a cold and blew
My nose giving oil to the arab world
I am so hip even my errors are correct
I sailed west to reach east and had to round off
    the earth as I went
    The hair from my head thinned and gold was laid
    across three continents

I am so perfect so divine so ethereal so surreal
I cannot be comprehended
    except by my permission

I mean…I…can fly
    like a bird in the sky…

Acknowledgments and Advisory Board

I do not believe anyone has 100 favorite anything…maybe peppermint pillows or chocolate candies, but those are the same, not different. I invited a poet, an actress, a scholar, and a young, upcoming poet to contribute ideas to this collection. Without the loving care of the Board of *The 100* Best African American Poems (*but I cheated)*…

Val Gray Ward, actress; founder of Kuumba Theatre of Chicago who is the Voice of the Harlem Renaissance

Mari Evans, award-winning poet and anthologist of *The Black Woman*

Dr. Joanne Gabbin, Director, Furious Flower Poetry Center at James Madison University

And my former student Kwame Alexander, award-winning poet; Director of the Washington DC Poetry Festival

…this labor of love would have been a chore rather than a pleasure. I cannot thank all of you enough for the help and guidance you offered.

—Nikki Giovanni, Winter 2010

About the Author

Nikki Giovanni is an award-winning poet, writer, and activist. She is the author of more than two dozen books for adults and children, including *Bicycles*, *Quilting the Black-Eyed Pea*, *Racism 101*, *Blues: For All the Changes*, and *Love Poems*. Her children's book-plus-audio compilation *Hip Hop Speaks to Children* was awarded the NAACP Image Award. Her children's book *Rosa*, a picture-book retelling of the Rosa Parks story, was a Caldecott Honor Book and winner of the Coretta Scott King Award. Both books were *New York Times* bestsellers. Nikki is a Grammy nominee for her spoken-word album *The Nikki Giovanni Poetry Collection* and has been nominated for the National Book Award. She has been voted Woman of the Year by *Essence*, *Mademoiselle*, and *Ladies' Home Journal*. She is a University Distinguished Professor at Virginia Tech, where she teaches writing and literature.

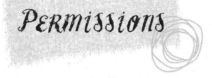

Permissions

Elizabeth Alexander: "Boston Year" from *Venus Hottentot*, copyright © 1990 by Elizabeth Alexander. Used with permission of Graywolf Press, www.graywolfpress.org.

Kwame Alexander: "Dancing Naked on the Floor" from *Dancing Naked on the Floor*, copyright © Kwame Alexander, reprinted by permission of the Writer's Lair Books; "Nikki, if you were a song...", copyright © Kwame Alexander, reprinted by permission of the author.

Asha Bandele: "from the center 2 the edge," reprinted by permission of the author; "the subtle art of breathing," copyright © Asha Bandele, reprinted by permission of the author and Moore Black Press.

Amiri Baraka (LeRoi Jones): "Ka'Ba" and "leroy" copyright © 1999 Amiri Baraka, William Harris. Reprinted by permission of Basic Books, a member of the Perseus Books Group.

Remica L. Bingham: "Marchers Headed for Washington, Baltimore, 1963," "Mercy Killing," "Things I Carried Coming Into the World," and "Topography" reprinted by permission of the author.

Nadir Lasana Bomani: untitled, reprinted by permission of the author.

Gwendolyn Brooks: "A Bronzeville Mother Loiters in Mississippi. Meanwhile, a Mississippi Mother Burns Bacon," "The Mother," "Sunset of the City," "The Last Quatrain of the Ballad of Emmett Till," "The Sermon on the Warpland," "We Real

Cool," and "When you have forgotten Sunday: the love story," reprinted by consent of Brooks Permissions.

Jericho Brown: "Autobiography" and "Beneath Me" from *Please*, reprinted by permission of New Issues Poetry & Prose.

Sterling A. Brown: "Old Lem" from *The Collected Poems of Sterling A. Brown*, selected by Michael S. Harper. Copyright © 1980 by Sterling A. Brown. Used by permission of HarperCollins Publishers.

Lucille Clifton: "homage to my hips," copyright © 1980 by Lucille Clifton. First appeared in *Two-Headed Woman*, published by the University of Massachusetts Press. Reprinted by permission of Curtis Brown, Ltd.; "i am accused of tending to the past" from *Quilting: Poems 1987–1990*. Copyright © 1991 by Lucille Clifton. Used with the permission of BOA Editions, Ltd., www.boaeditions.org.

Countee Cullen: "Heritage," "Incident," and "Yet Do I Marvel," copyrights held by Amistad Research Center, Tulane University; administered by Thompson and Thompson, Brooklyn, New York.

Fred D'Aguiar: "A Clean Slate," copyright © Fred D'Aguiar, from *Continental Shelf* (2009), used by permission of Carcanet Press Limited.

Adam Daniel: "I fade into the night," reprinted by permission of the author.

Kwame Dawes: "Train Ride," copyright © Kwame Dawes, from *Wisteria*, reprinted by permission of Red Hen Press.

Toi Derricotte: "Before Making Love" from *Captivity* by Toi Derricotte, copyright © 1989. Reprinted by permission of the University of Pittsburgh Press.

DJ Renegade: "Haiku" and "That And Some Mo'" reprinted by permission of the author.

Rita Dove: "Sunday Greens" from *Selected Poems*, copyright © 1993 by Rita Dove, reprinted by permission of Random House, Inc.

Camille T. Dungy: "Cleaning," copyright © Camille T. Dungy, from *What to Eat, What to Drink, What to Leave for Poison*, reprinted by permission of Red Hen Press.

Cornelius Eady: "The Supremes" from *The Gathering of My Name*. Copyright © 1991 by Cornelius Eady. Reprinted with the permission of Carnegie Mellon University Press, www.cmu.edu/universitypress.

Thomas Sayers Ellis: "All Their Stanzas Look Alike" and "View of the Library of Congress from Paul Laurence Dunbar High School" from *The Maverick Room*. opyright © 2005 by Thomas Sayers Ellis. Used with the permission of Graywolf Press, Minneapolis, Minnesota, www.graywolfpress.org.

Mari Evans: "I Am a Black Woman," "The Aunt," and "Who Can Be Born Black?" reprinted by permission of the author.

Nikky Finney: "The Girlfriend's Train," reprinted by permission of the author.

Ruth Forman: "Poetry Should Ride the Bus" from *We Are the Young Musicians*, copyright © 1993 by Ruth Forman. Reprinted by permission of Beacon Press, Boston.

Nikki Giovanni: "And Yeah...This is A Love Poem" from *Love Poems* by Nikki Giovanni, copyright © 1968–1997 by Nikki Giovanni, reprinted by permission of HarperCollins Publishers; "Bicycles" from *Bicycles: Love Poems* by Nikki Giovanni, copyright © 2009 by Nikki Giovanni, reprinted by permission of HarperCollins Publishers; "Ego Tripping" from *The Selected Poems of Nikki Giovanni* by Nikki Giovanni, copyright © 1996 by Nikki Giovanni, reprinted by permission of HarperCollins Publishers; "Knoxville, Tennessee" and "Nikki-Rosa" from *Black Feeling, Black Talk, Black Judgment* by Nikki Giovanni, copyright © 1968, 1970 by Nikki Giovanni, reprinted by permission of HarperCollins Publishers; "Train Rides" from *Blues: For All the Changes* by Nikki Giovanni, copyright © 1999 by Nikki Giovanni, reprinted by permission of HarperCollins Publishers.

Antoine Harris: "Jazz Baby is it in you," reprinted by permission of the author.

Robert Hayden: "Frederick Douglass," and "Those Winter Sundays" copyright © 1966 by Robert Hayden from *Collected Poems of Robert Hayden* by Robert Hayden, edited by Frederick Glaysher. Used by permission of Liveright Corporation.

Terrance Hayes: "The Blue Terrance: I come from a long line hollowed out on a dry night," from *Wind in a Box* by Terrance Hayes, copyright © 2006 by Terrance Hayes. Used by permission of Penguin, a division of Penguin Group (USA), Inc.

Akua Lezli Hope: "Song Through the Wall," reprinted by permission of the author.

Langston Hughes: "Dream Boogie," "Dream Boogie: Variation," "Easy Boogie," "Good Morning," "Harlem," "Island," "The Negro Speaks of Rivers," "Same in Blues," and "Theme for English B" from *The Collected Poems of Langston Hughes* by Langston Hughes, copyright © 1994 by The Estate of Langston Hughes. Used by permission of Alfred A. Knopf, a division of Random House, Inc.

Index